W9-BAP-315

SOLDIER'S COURAGE
The Story of Stephen Crane

SOLDIER'S COURAGE
The Story of Stephen Crane

Bonnie L. Lukes

620 South Elm Street, Suite 223
Greensboro, North Carolina   27406
http://www.morganreynolds.com

SOLDIER'S COURAGE: THE STORY OF STEPHEN CRANE

Copyright © 2002 by Bonnie L. Lukes

Library of Congress Cataloging-in-Publication Data

Lukes, Bonnie L.
  Soldier's courage : the story of Stephen Crane / Bonnie L. Lukes.—
1st ed.
      p. cm.
Includes bibliographical references and index.
  ISBN 1-883846-94-3 (library binding)
  1. Crane, Stephen, 1871-1900—Juvenile literature. 2.   Authors,
American—19th century—Biography—Juvenile literature.   I. Title.
  PS1449.C85 Z734 2002
  813'.4—dc21

                              2002005095

Printed in the United States of America
First Edition

To Kathleen, loyal friend and mentor.

Contents

Stephen Crane, 1899.
(Courtesy of Syracuse University)

Chapter One

Preacher's Kid

Stephen Crane lived his life as if he knew he did not have much time. He wrote his first novel when he was only twenty-one and published his masterpiece, *The Red Badge of Courage*, at twenty-three. By age twenty-five, he was a well-known feature writer and correspondent for a large newspaper syndicate. He was dead before his twenty-ninth birthday.

Crane's life is a study in contradiction. At times he seemed bent on self-destruction; at other times he exhibited a dogged determination to survive. His contemporaries spoke of looking for the "real" Stephen Crane. Those who knew him best often suspected they did not know him at all.

From beginning to end of his short life, he displayed an inborn irreverence for authority, thumbed his nose at conventional society, and was determined to walk his own path. "I expect to make a sincere, desperate, lonely battle to remain true to my conception of my life and the way it should be lived . . ." he wrote a friend. He did so, but the price he paid was high.

Stephen Crane was born on November 1, 1871, in a Methodist parsonage at Fourteen Mulberry Place in Newark, New Jersey. He was the fourteenth and last child of the Reverend Jonathon Townley Crane and Mary Helen Peck Crane. His middle-aged parents—Mrs. Crane was forty-five and Reverend Crane was fifty-two—had not anticipated having another child. Nevertheless, Reverend Crane serenely noted that day in his journal: "This morning . . . our fourteenth child was born. We call him Stephen, the name of the ancestor . . . of Revolutionary times, who was prominent in patriotic labors and counsels."

Only eight of the thirteen Crane children born before Stephen—six brothers and two sisters—survived to welcome him into the family. Because of the age differences between Stephen and his siblings—the oldest was twenty-one, and the youngest was eight—he grew up almost like an only child.

Stephen's family was steeped in religion. Reverend Crane, who had a doctor of divinity degree, served as the presiding elder over sixteen Methodist churches in the Newark district. In addition, he authored numerous religious tracts about the dangers of using tobacco, opium, and alcohol. He also wrote a number of books. One book, titled *Popular Amusements,* written two years before Stephen's birth, warned against reading novels because they generate a "morbid love of excitement."

Stephen's father, Reverend Jonathan Townley Crane, was a stern man who preached against reading novels and other such "amusements." *(Courtesy of Syracuse University)*

Despite his stern ideas (he also disapproved of dancing, card playing, and baseball), Reverend Crane was a gentle, idealistic man with a sense of humor. "He liked all kinds of animals," Stephen recalled, adding with sly wit that his father "never drove a horse faster than two yards an hour even if some Christian was dying elsewhere." Stephen shared this love of animals, especially horses. Horseback riding became one of his great joys. "I . . . think a good saddle-horse is the one blessing of life," he once said.

On his mother's side, Stephen declared that "everybody as soon as he could walk became a Methodist clergyman." Mary Helen Crane (called Helen) was the daughter of a minister and the niece of a bishop. She lectured, wrote for Methodist papers, and was active in the Women's Christian Temperance Union, an organization that opposed the sale and use of alcohol.

Of his mother, Stephen later wrote:

> [She] was a very religious woman but I don't think that she was as narrow [in her thinking] as most of her friends or her family . . . My brothers tell me that she got herself into trouble [with the Methodist community] . . . by taking care of a girl who had an accidental baby . . . But mother was always more of a Christian than a Methodist and she kept this girl at our house . . . until she found [her] a home somewhere.

Stephen also boasted about his mother's efforts to change the role of women in public schools. "One of my

Helen Crane was active in the temperance movement.
(Courtesy of Syracuse University)

sisters was a teacher and mother tried for years to get women placed on the school boards." However, the ladies in Dr. Crane's congregation were less impressed. Shocked by Mrs. Crane's indifferent housekeeping, they informed her that "she ought to stay at home and take care of her large family, instead of making so many speeches."

Despite his parents' active lives, Stephen's early childhood was not much different from that of most boys—especially those with older brothers. The family spent summers at Ocean Grove, a Methodist retreat on the New Jersey coast. Stephen's brother Edmund recalled that when Stephen was not yet four, he and his brothers often took him swimming in the river. Edmund told how once, Stephen, "started to [swim] to . . . my . . . brother, who was farther out in the river. As the depth gradually increased the water came up to his chin, then to his mouth, and then his eyes, but he kept steadily on, and, I plucked him out, gasping but [not] scared, just as his yellow hair was going under. We boys were naturally delighted with his grit."

Stephen's sister Agnes, who was planning to be a teacher, taught him to read and write. Despite Reverend Crane's disapproval of novels, Agnes boasted that by the age of four Stephen was reading James Fenimore Cooper. According to Edmund, Stephen also displayed an early interest in writing—even before he knew the alphabet.

"Stevie was making weird marks on a paper with a lead pencil one day," Edmund recalled, "and in the

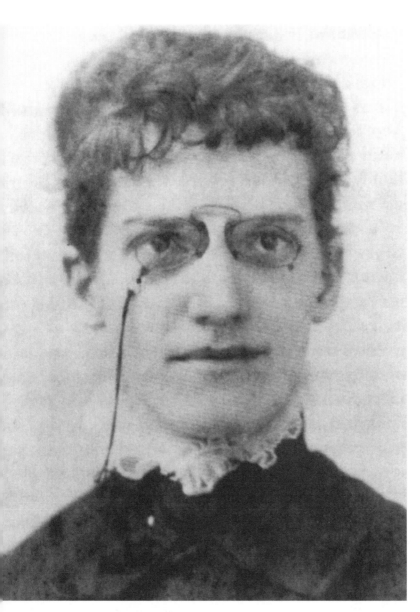

Stephen felt especially close to his older sister Agnes.
(Courtesy of Syracuse University)

exact tone of one, absorbed in composition, and coming to the surface only for a moment for needed information, called to his mother, 'Ma, how do you spell 'O'?' "

Agnes probably encouraged her brother's early faltering attempts to write stories. None of these first efforts has survived other than a four-stanza poem written when he was eight or nine. The poem reveals a child's disdain for clothes as Christmas gifts:

> Last Christmas they gave me a sweater,
> And a nice warm suit of wool,
> But I'd rather be cold and have a dog,
> To watch when I come from school.

In April 1878, when Stephen was six years old, Reverend Crane was appointed pastor of Drew Methodist Church in the rural village of Port Jervis, New York.

Port Jervis became the place Stephen always considered home. A small boy could roam over its rolling, pine-covered hills, exploring and dreaming—making every tree a soldier and every rock a fortress to be stormed. Directly to the north was Sullivan County, where Stephen would camp, hunt, fish, and ride horses with his brothers and friends. Its hills and valleys later served as models for landscapes described in his early stories as well as in *The Red Badge of Courage.*

Stephen started public school just before his seventh birthday, but frequent illnesses prevented him from completing his first year. In March 1879, when his health improved, he again enrolled in first grade.

Stephen quickly made up for lost time. "They tell me that I got through two grades in six weeks which sounds like the lie of a fond mother at a tea party," he later recalled, "but I do remember that I got ahead very fast and that father was pleased with me." Whether he owed his swift progress to Agnes's tutoring, or to an eight-year-old's humiliation at being put in the same grade as five- and six-year-olds, is unknown.

Chapter Two

Leaving Home

On Monday, February 16, 1880, Stephen's world turned upside down when his father unexpectedly died. The day before, Reverend Crane had preached for his congregation as usual. The next day, he complained of feeling ill. A doctor was summoned, but nothing could be done. The official cause of death was listed as heart failure. However, Stephen said later that the family thought "he worked himself to death."

Stephen never spoke about the pain of losing his father, but years later he still cherished memories of times they had spent together. "He used to take me driving with him to little places near Port Jervis where he was going to preach or bury somebody. Once we got mixed up in an Irish funeral near a place named Slate Hill. Everybody was drunk and father was scandalized . . . He was so [innocent] and good that I often think he didn't know much of anything about humanity."

Soon after her husband's death, Helen Crane had to

vacate the Methodist parsonage. She moved to Roseville, a town near Newark. For reasons that are unclear, she left Stephen in the care of his brother Edmund, who was teaching school in Sussex, New Jersey. Although Stephen never acknowledged it, this separation from his mother and the familiar comforts of home so soon after losing his father must have troubled him.

Helen returned three months later. Her son William, fresh out of law school, had returned to Port Jervis to set up a law practice, and Helen and Stephen moved in with him. Agnes also graduated and began teaching at Mountain House School, where Stephen was a student. For the next three years, Stephen's life remained stable.

Then in the summer of 1883, when he was eleven, his mother moved them to Asbury Park, 120 miles away from Port Jervis. Asbury Park was a resort town on the New Jersey coast, just a mile away from Ocean Grove, where the family had vacationed.

The two towns presented a bewildering contrast to a young boy. In Ocean Grove, known as "The Summer Mecca of Methodist Americans," alcohol, tobacco, and Sunday newspapers were prohibited along with the daring, new-style bathing suits fashionable for women. Asbury Park, however, offered glamorous, glittering hotels and an "anything goes" atmosphere.

But Helen Crane had not moved to Asbury Park on a whim. Almost immediately, she was elected president of the Asbury Park and Ocean Grove Women's Christian Temperance Union (WCTU). Soon she was giving lectures, writing for Methodist newspapers, and holding temperance meetings. Occasionally, she traveled to distant cities as a delegate for the WCTU. Stephen said that after his father died, his mother "lived in and for religion."

Stephen's brother Townley and his wife Fannie also lived in Asbury Park. Nineteen years older than Stephen, Townley published the *Newark Advertiser*. He also operated an agency that supplied news items to the *New York Tribune*, the *New York Sun*, and the Associated Press. Helen occasionally contributed religious news to her son's agency.

Before long, Agnes left her teaching job in Port Jervis and secured another in Asbury Park. Now twenty-seven and unmarried, she moved in with her mother and helped her care for Stephen.

Stephen began sixth grade in September, and shortly afterwards the family suffered the first in a series of misfortunes. In November, Townley's wife Fannie died of Bright's disease. One year later, Agnes became so ill she had to resign from her teaching position. She died on June 10, 1884, of cerebrospinal meningitis. She was only twenty-eight years old.

Stephen was twelve when Agnes died. She had been a comforting, steadfast presence in his life, and her death left a painful void. But with his usual reticence about such things, he never recorded his feelings.

In school, he maintained a respectable, if not outstanding, grade average. He also developed a passion for baseball. During the summer, he played for the Asbury Park team. Even though Stephen was one of the team's youngest and smallest players, word began to get around that "no one in Asbury Park could throw a ball he could not catch bare-handed."

At thirteen or fourteen, Stephen wrote his earliest known short story, "Uncle Jake and the Bell Handle," a comical tale about a country bumpkin and his first trip to the city. The story shows glimpses of a budding talent. However, Stephen was more interested in playing baseball than in writing stories. He wrote to a friend that he wanted to be a professional baseball player, but then added cheerfully: "Ma says it's not a serious occupation and Will says I have to go to college first."

In September 1885, a little over a year after Agnes's death, Helen enrolled Stephen at Pennington Seminary, a Methodist Academy his father had helped to found. Pennington was a boarding school located seven miles north of Trenton. The school's principal purpose was to prepare young men for the ministry. Religious services were held in the school chapel twice daily, and attendance was compulsory. On Sunday, students were required to attend services at a church in the village. In addition, Sunday Bible classes were held in the chapel, and prayer meetings took place every Wednesday night.

The Pennington curriculum stressed language, literature, history, and English composition. The school also maintained a vigorous athletic department with emphasis on football and baseball. There is no existing evidence that Stephen participated in either of these sports, but it is probable that he did.

In September 1886, at the beginning of his second

year at Pennington, Stephen learned that his brother Luther had been killed in a freak accident. At age twenty-three, Luther was the closest to Stephen in age. He was also the third family member to die within six years.

The summer following Luther's death, Stephen, at age fifteen, experienced for the first time the exhilaration of seeing his own words in print. An Asbury Park newspaper published an unsigned, three-hundred-word sketch that he had written.

In the fall, Stephen began his third year at the seminary. However, he never completed it. About a month before the Christmas holiday break, a teacher accused him of hazing [harassing] another student. Stephen denied it. When the teacher refused to believe him, Stephen packed his bags and went home. "As the professor called me a liar," he explained to his family, "there was not room in Pennington for us both."

His brother Wilbur later recalled that, "Nothing would induce him to return to the seminary. Stephen's most marked characteristic was his absolute truthfulness. He was in many minor scrapes but no consideration of consequences would induce him to lie out of them."

Stephen had always been fascinated with war, and he now decided he wanted a military career. As a result, his mother enrolled him at the Claverack College and Hudson River Institute located in New York state's Hudson River Valley. Claverack was a semi-military institution that would prepare him for West Point. Like Pennington, the school strongly emphasized religion.

Claverack was a Methodist co-educational school

Stephen Crane as a cadet at Claverack College in 1889.
(Courtesy of Syracuse University)

that had once enjoyed a reputation for high academic standards. However, after merging with the Hudson River Institute, the school's standards dropped considerably. According to Stephen's classmate Harvey Wickhim, "Students roamed . . . like packs of cheerful wolves out of bounds, out of hours and very much out of hand."

But Stephen would describe his time at Claverack as "the happiest period of my life." He started there in January 1888, first enrolling in classical courses, then switching to an academic program that included physiology, English literature, history, and grammar. Grammar was his worst subject, and he never fully mastered it. He later said of the college: "I never learned anything there . . . But heaven was sunny blue and no rain fell on the diamond when I was playing baseball. I was very happy, there."

At Claverack he displayed his dual personality. On the one hand, Stephen delighted in the daily military drills, soon earning the rank of corporal. On the other, his dress and conduct outside of the military aspect were often unconventional. As a result, friends and classmates differed in their perceptions of him: some described him as fun loving, while others saw him as aloof and withdrawn. One friend, Tommy Borland, probably came closest to the truth when he pronounced Stephen "a law unto himself."

Perhaps it was a desire to avoid the mocking label of "preacher's kid" that made Stephen determined to acquire a "bad boy" reputation. Yet, while he smoked cigarettes and used strong language, he steered clear of

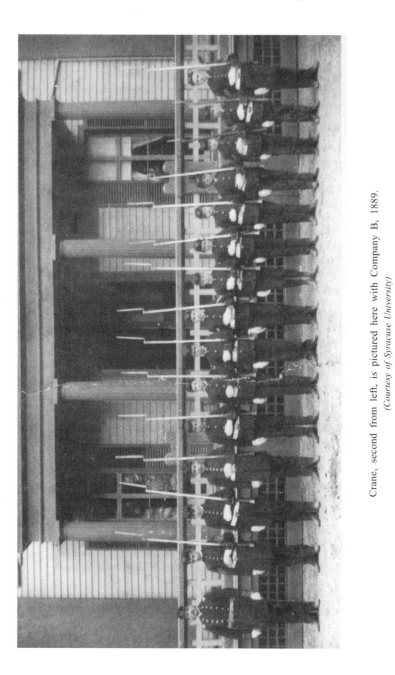

Crane, second from left, is pictured here with Company B, 1889.
(Courtesy of Syracuse University)

more serious offenses. As one classmate noted, "his name was never among those read out at morning chapel."

During his first semester at Claverack, he had a crush on a different girl every week. After he achieved fame, a woman who had been a classmate wrote him requesting a copy of his book *Red Badge of Courage*. In his response, he wrote: "Of course, you were joking . . . that I might not remember you. And Anna Roberts! And Eva Lacy! And Jennie Pierce! . . . Jennie was clever. With only half an effort she made my life so very miserable."

According to the *Asbury Park Daily Press*, Stephen returned home for the summer of 1888 wearing "the stripes of a corporal on his natty uniform." That summer, he had his first reporting experience. By this time, his brother Townley had achieved a solid reputation as a newspaperman, and he gave Stephen the task of gathering resort news for him. Stephen received no byline. Whatever items Townley chose to publish appeared in print unsigned.

When Stephen returned to Claverack in the fall, drill training continued to hold his interest. He proved to be a capable drillmaster and was promoted to first lieutenant that semester. But other than the drills, he devoted most of his energy to baseball, playing catcher barehanded until his sore hands forced him to use a glove. Ignoring his mother's stern warnings, Stephen squandered time hanging around pool halls and billiard rooms. But in his usual paradoxical way, he also sang in the Methodist choir.

In February 1890, the school newspaper, *Vidette*, published an essay Stephen had written on the explorer Henry Stanley. Although the writing was not inspired, it was his first signed publication. Also that spring, he was elected captain of the baseball team. True to form and without any explanation, he refused the honor, passing it on to the first baseman. When Stephen left Claverack for summer vacation, he looked forward to returning in the fall.

His family, however, had other plans for him. They decided that because the family owned stock in a Pennsylvania coal mine, he should transfer to Lafayette College in Easton, Pennsylvania, and study mining engineering. It is hard to believe that Stephen was happy with this arrangement, but there is no record showing that he resisted. He worked for Townley throughout summer vacation, and in the fall, he boarded a train to Lafayette College.

He enrolled in courses on Milton, the Bible, geometry, algebra, industrial drawing, chemistry and French. Perhaps in an effort to survive the school's rigid atmosphere, Stephen joined Lafayette's largest fraternity, Delta Upsilon. He also joined two literary clubs that sponsored frequent lectures and debates and had access to current books.

Stephen had not openly rebelled against going to Lafayette, but once there, he seldom attended classes. It was not baseball season, but he hung around the diamond anyway, participating in pickup games every afternoon. Sometimes he and his friends played pool and talked about literature.

Stephen missed Claverack and his friends there. He replied to a friend who had complained about Claverack: "Mark my words, you will always regret the day you leave old [Claverack College]." Sounding forlorn and lonely, he closed the letter, "So long, old man, don't forget me even if I can't be at C.C."

At the end of the semester, Stephen had failed five of his seven courses, including theme writing, for which he received a zero. (The themes were on technical subjects assigned by the engineering faculty.) "I found mining and engineering not at all to my taste. I preferred baseball," Crane said. A classmate remarked, "We all counted on him to make the baseball team in the spring [but] . . . he quietly took his departure."

Before Stephen left Lafayette, he wrote his brother Edmund to say that he had decided on a literary career. It was the first time he had acknowledged such an ambition. He asked his brother for help in convincing their mother to let him change his course of study. Helen Crane did not object.

In January 1891, having turned nineteen in November, Stephen enrolled at Syracuse University in upstate New York. He arrived at the Delta Upsilon fraternity house "in a cab and cloud of tobacco smoke." By this time he was a chain smoker.

He enrolled as a non-degree student in the College of Liberal Arts and registered for only one course, English literature. His baseball reputation had preceded him. The school newspaper noted, "Crane . . . has entered the University and will make a good addition to

Crane (front row, middle) was an asset to the Syracuse University baseball team.
(Courtesy of Syracuse University)

the [baseball] team." Stephen had no trouble making the varsity team, and later confessed that he had attended Syracuse "more to play baseball than to study." He was the team's catcher, although he occasionally played shortstop.

The shortstop position would have been more suited to his physique; he was only about five-foot-eight and lean. A teammate described him as "small-chested and droop-shouldered, with unruly white-blond hair, yellow skin, and cool blue-gray eyes." He lacked the arm strength needed for a catcher, but his will and determination more than compensated for any weakness. He was a good hitter, carrying an average of .300 or better in his first six games. His teammates elected him captain of the team, a high honor for a freshman.

Stephen's strong will extended beyond the baseball field. Once when he openly disagreed with the university president, the president tried to shame him by invoking the Bible. "What does St. Paul say, Mr. Crane," the president asked, "What does St. Paul say?" Stephen retorted, "I know what St. Paul says, but I disagree with St. Paul." When an upperclassman ordered him to "turn grindstone for [sharpening] the kitchen knives," Stephen snapped that he "never had and never would turn grindstone for anybody."

Overall, however, Stephen was much happier at Syracuse than at Lafayette, although he still did very little studying. Townley had arranged for him to act as Syracuse's local correspondent for the *Tribune*, and Stephen took the job seriously. "When I ought to have been at [class]," he remembered later, "I was studying faces on the streets . . . and watching the trains roll in and out of Central Station." He hung around the police station and observed the prisoners being brought in by the police. His close friend and fraternity brother Frederic Lawrence later said, "His future was in literature, and never for an instant did he doubt his own success."

Stephen and Frederic, with other friends and fraternity brothers, defied school rules by keeping late hours, attending the theater, and playing poker in their rooms. But Stephen also spent a lot of time in Thomas Durston's bookstore, where he discovered the books of Russian novelist Leo Tolstoy. He read *Anna Karenina* and *War and Peace* that spring and began to take his own writing more seriously. While his fraternity brothers attended classes, he remained in his room reading history and literary classics—often until late at night. His first published story, "The King's Favor," appeared in the university's literary magazine in May.

Stephen went home to Asbury Park after the spring term ended. He would never return to the university. His formal education was finished. He later recalled: "I did little work at school, but confined my abilities, such as they were, to the diamond. Not that I disliked books, but the cut and dried curriculum of the college did not appeal to me. Humanity was a much more interesting study."

Chapter Three

Lessons of Asbury Park

Back in Asbury Park, Stephen worked full-time for Townley's news service. But first he joined friends Frederic Lawrence and Louis Senger on a camping trip in the rugged woods of Sullivan County, New York. Spending time in the outdoors with close friends was Stephen's favorite way to relax and refresh his spirit. In between the hunting and fishing, he talked to the local residents and listened intently to their stories, sometimes even taking notes. He called them "wonderful yarn spinners."

Out of these tales would come his Sullivan County sketches, several of which the *New York Tribune* published the following year. They began as journalistic essays but soon evolved into fiction. Often humorous, the sketches reflected Mark Twain's influence on the young writer. Some of the darker ones, however, were reminiscent of Edgar Allan Poe. These Stephen called his "little grotesque tales of the woods." This early writing was frequently awkward, but the ironic tone that would characterize his future fiction was already evident.

Stephen left the woods and returned to Asbury Park just as the summer resort crowd descended on the town. "The beach, the avenues and the shaded lawns are once more covered with the bright-hued garments of the summer throng," he wrote.

Assigned by Townley to write local color pieces, he covered both Asbury Park and Ocean Grove as well as Avon-by-the-Sea, the nearby culture center. Avon attracted prominent artists and lecturers.

Much of Stephen's work was still printed unsigned, making it difficult to determine exactly how many pieces he published that summer. He put in many hours of writing every day—not just writing pieces for Townley, but also writing fiction.

When Stephen told his brother that he wished to have a professional's opinion of his stories, Townley introduced him to William Fletcher Johnson, the *New York Tribune's* day editor. Stephen showed Johnson two of his Sullivan County sketches, and the editor accepted them both for publication in the *New York Tribune's* Sunday supplement.

Such positive affirmation of his work was gratifying, but Stephen craved something more. He was seeking his own voice, feeling his way toward a new kind of literary expression that he could neither fully explain nor define. On August 17, 1891, he covered a lecture at Avon that would help him in that search.

The speaker was Hamlin Garland, who had just published his first book. Garland was also a regular contributor to some of the nation's best literary magazines, among them the highly regarded *Harper's Weekly*. His lecture—one of a series on literature that he delivered during July and August—was on William Dean Howells, a popular novelist and respected editor and critic.

Both Garland and Howells—unlike earlier novelists—felt that novels should present real-life situations, or what Howells described as "the truthful treatment of commonplace material." This style of writing, called realism, even advocated reproducing colloquial speech in dialogue.

For Crane, hearing someone such as Garland put into words theories that he himself had already vaguely formulated but had been unable to articulate, was a thrilling, spine-tingling moment. Crane said later that he thought he had developed "all alone a little creed of art," only to discover that his "creed was identical with the one of Howells and Garland." In Crane's report on the lecture, he wrote, "[Howells] stands for all that is progressive and humanitarian in our fiction."

Soon after this experience, Stephen joined his friends for a second camping trip, this time to Pike County, Pennsylvania. "Crane loved this [outdoor] life, and his health was magnificent," Frederic Lawrence would recall. "As the month wore on, exposure to the sun gave his skin a copper color almost like that of an American Indian, and it formed a strange contrast to his still light hair."

The camping trip ended about the same time vaca-tioners were leaving Asbury Park. Stephen left too, mov-ing in with his brother Edmund in the Lake View suburb of Patterson, New Jersey. Edmund's home was within easy commuting distance of New York City, and from there, Stephen—probably as a result of hearing Gar-land—began his first explorations of the Bowery.

The Bowery was a tawdry area of southeast Manhat-tan made up of saloons, dance halls, brothels, and flop-houses that offered a cheap room for the night. Stephen could lose himself in the masses of people, and study "the bums and outcasts . . . standing in the rain like chickens in a storm." It may have been about this time that he began a rough draft for a novel about a young prostitute named Maggie.

On December 7, 1891, shortly after Stephen's twen-tieth birthday, his mother died. He had suffered many losses in his young life, and her death completed the circle. Again he kept any sorrow confined within him-self.

He continued to live with Edmund and to spend much of his time exploring the Bowery. He sometimes stayed overnight in one of the cheap hotels, partly to experience the life of the homeless, and partly because it was all he could afford. He had no fixed income, and meals were hit and miss; sometimes he ate, sometimes he did not. He borrowed money from friends when he could, and if he desperately needed a warm meal and a place to sleep, he returned to Edmund's house.

Stephen wrote more Sullivan County sketches, which

the *Tribune* continued to publish on a freelance basis. At the same time, he sought steady employment as a journalist. He made the rounds of all the New York newspapers: the *Tribune*, *Times*, *Sun*, and *World*. But the editors refused to hire him, probably because of his youth and inexperience. Discouraged, Stephen returned to Asbury Park in June of 1892 to begin another summer of reporting resort activities for Townley and the *Tribune*.

During his twentieth summer, Stephen fell in love with Lily Brandon Monroe, a slightly older woman. Unfortunately for Stephen, she was married, although the marriage apparently was not a happy one. Those who knew Lily described her as "bewitchingly lovely." She had the kind of golden blond hair that always attracted Stephen. His nieces had that same color hair, and Stephen had told them that if he ever found a woman with hair like theirs, he would marry her.

The attraction between Lily and Stephen was strong and immediate. They spent hours strolling along the boardwalk, riding the merry-go-round at the amusement park, and taking long walks along the shore, watching the waves roll in. He told her that in the future, "whenever she saw the ocean she would think of him."

To further complicate the romance, Lily came from a wealthy family who did not approve of Stephen. In truth he had little to offer her. He gave her the only thing of value that he possessed—some of his manuscripts. He begged her to leave her husband and elope with him. Lily was tempted, but she ultimately refused.

In a short story written less than a year later, Stephen made its ending fit his dreams. The story, titled "The Pace of Youth," is set in an amusement park. The impoverished young man who runs the merry-go-round falls in love with the owner's daughter. He convinces her to elope with him. The daughter's character was clearly modeled after Lily.

Stephen's burning infatuation with Lily did not interfere with his writing. Throughout that spring and summer, more Sullivan County sketches appeared in the *Tribune*. In July, the paper published his first New York sketch called "Travels in New York: The Broken-Down Van," a story that had grown out of his Bowery explorations. He also continued to write about local events for Townley, short pieces in which he often ridiculed the resort life of Asbury Park.

In August, Townley assigned Stephen to cover a parade of the Junior Order of United American Mechanics, an association of patriotic working men. His subsequent article, printed in the *Tribune*, offended many people. He ridiculed the mechanics' marching style and mocked the well-to-do spectators with their "summer gowns, lace parasols, tennis trousers, straw hats and indifferent smiles."

"The bona fide Asbury Parker," he wrote with scorching sarcasm, "is a man to whom a dollar, when held close to his eye, often shuts out any impression . . . that other people possess rights." Then, for good measure, he criticized the resort community itself. "[It] creates nothing. It does not make; it merely amuses."

Angry union members wrote to the *Tribune*, calling the piece "un-American" and demanding an apology. Stephen had not meant to offend the workers. He had intended to show the irony of wealthy men and women turning out to watch a parade of common workers.

However, the damage was done. The *Tribune* was forced to print a retraction, but this was not all that angered the publisher. The paper's owner was running for vice-president on the Republican ticket, and he did not want the *Tribune* perceived as anti-working class. A few more of Stephen's pieces were printed, but after 1892, nothing of his was ever again published in the *Tribune*. And the paper would "[seize] upon every opportunity to revile him for the remainder of his career."

The *Asbury Park Daily Press* added its own criticism of Crane. "This young man has a hankering for razzle-dazzle style . . . The article was in bad taste, unworthy [of] a reputable reporter."

When asked if he regretted writing the piece, Crane responded: "No! You've got to feel the things you write if you want to make an impact on the world."

Shortly after this scandal, the writer Hamlin Garland returned to Asbury Park. Garland was only a few years older than Stephen, and on this second meeting, the two men discovered they shared common interests. During Garland's stay, they played baseball and discussed literature. Stephen also showed Garland his first attempt at a novel, an early draft of what would ultimately be called *Maggie: A Girl of the Streets*.

Garland gave him a letter of introduction to Richard

Watson Gilder, the editor of *Century Illustrated Magazine*. "I want you to read a *great* [manuscript] of Stephen Crane's making," Garland wrote. "I think him an astonishing fellow. And [I] have advised him to bring the [manuscript] to you."

Apparently, Crane was not yet satisfied with the novel because he did not show it to Gilder at that time. Instead, during September and October of 1892, he worked for the *Newark Advertiser*. But he was growing restless with this kind of journalism. He wanted to take his writing to another level. He wanted to write literature, and it seemed to him that the only place to do that was in New York.

Chapter Four

Maggie's Town

Nearly half a century before Stephen Crane set out for New York City, Henry David Thoreau left his home in Concord, Massachusetts, and moved to Walden Pond. On his third day at Walden, he wrote in his journal: "I wish to meet the facts of life . . . face to face, And so I came . . . here. Life! who knows what it is?"

Crane went to the much larger New York City for the same reason. "I decided," he said, "that the nearer a writer gets to life the greater he becomes as an artist."

The last few decades of the nineteenth century, with the rapid industrialization and widening gap between the wealthy and the poor in America, would be labeled the "guilded age" by Mark Twain. By the 1890s, the rapid growth of big cities had resulted in rampant political corruption. Violent labor strikes rocked the cities, and the bleak, harsh living conditions in city slums sparked reform movements throughout the nation.

Literature, as well as other arts, reflected this unrest.

A cultural literary war erupted between the realist writers and the romantics. As the term implies, realists wrote about all aspects of life, including the ugly and the sordid, while the romantic writers tended to focus on creating a deeper illusion. Most Americans preferred the latter. Western adventure stories, romances, and ten-cent thrillers outsold realistic novels four to one.

Nowhere was the national unrest and discontent more evident than in New York City, when Stephen Crane—rebellious and eager to discard all the old rules—arrived in October 1892. He moved into a shabby rooming house occupied by a group of medical students. His old friend and college roommate Frederic Lawrence, now studying medicine, lived there. The house was located between the Bowery and the East River, and Crane and Lawrence shared a room that overlooked the water. Stephen nicknamed the band of young men "The Pendennis Club."

According to Lawrence, it was in this house that Crane began a major revision of *Maggie*. "As the story, a sordid tale of life in the tenements and the underworld took shape . . . [Stephen] became enthusiastic," Lawrence recalled. "[And] we sallied forth into the mean streets and dangerous neighborhoods in search of the local color that would give life to the great work."

The grimy streets of crowded Manhattan were a far cry from the breezy shores of Asbury Park. Horse-drawn trucks, vans, and cabs jammed the cobbled streets. On the sidewalks, the teeming throngs hurried along.

Young boys, sent by their fathers to purchase beer, squirmed their way through the crowd balancing foaming pitchers or pails. Young women hired by shopkeepers to "pull in" customers stood outside clothing store doors. Newsboys, trying to sell their papers, shouted out the current headlines. Police patrolled the streets both on foot and on horseback. Men carried signs for restaurants advertising "Breakfast 13 cents; Dinner, 15 cents." Liquor stores offered "Hot spiced rum, 6 cents; Sherry with a Big Egg in it, 5 cents."

As Crane soaked up the sights and sounds of the city, Maggie and her star-crossed life became more and more real to him. Meanwhile, in December, one of his Sullivan County stories, "A Tent in Agony," was published in *Cosmopolitan*. It marked Crane's first appearance in a popular magazine.

Sometime during the winter of 1892-93, Stephen showed the *Maggie* manuscript—along with Garland's letter of recommendation—to Richard Gilder at *Century Magazine*. Stephen thought Gilder might be intrigued because the story was set in the slums, and Gilder was interested in tenement reform. Gilder had published several essays deploring the squalor and poverty that typified the slums, but *Maggie* was too controversial for him. A conservative at heart, Gilder was shocked by the profanity in the book and by its candid chronicling of prostitution. "You mean that the story's too honest," Crane reportedly told him.

There is no indication that Crane tried to interest another publisher in *Maggie*. Instead, he decided to

Crane self-published his first novel, *Maggie: A Girl of the Streets*, under the pseudonym Johnston Smith.

have it privately printed. Two events enabled him to do this. In January 1893, his brother William bought Stephen's one-seventh share in their mother's house in Asbury Park, and that same month Stephen sold William his shares in the Pennsylvania coal mine. He used these two small sums of money to pay a printer.

On January 19, he requested his book to be catalogued by the Library of Congress. The title page read: "A Girl of the Streets,/A Story of New York./—By—/ Stephen Crane." (The name "Maggie" would be added to the title later.)

It was also in January that Crane met Corwin Knapp Linson, a painter and illustrator. Linson had a studio on the southwest corner of Broadway and Thirtieth Street. The young men became friends, and Crane spent many hours there, often writing while Linson painted. "Steve reveled in the use of words as a painter loves his color," Linson said. "To create unusual images with them . . . was as natural [to him] as to eat when meal time came."

"In memory . . ." Linson wrote later, "I see a pair of serene blue eyes and a quiet smile that lights the whole of a face . . . The sound of his voice comes to me, and the quick turn of the body, but it is the smile that lingers."

In late February or early March 1893, *Maggie: A Girl of the Streets* appeared in print. The book's cover was an unattractive mustard color, and the author's name appeared as "Johnston Smith." Frederic Lawrence said that Stephen used a penname because he "wished to disguise the authorship of a book that would offend his prudish relatives." Linson said that Crane told him the alias was mere chance, that it was the "commonest name I could think of . . . and no one could find me in the mob of Smiths."

In any event, the book appeared in print priced at fifty cents a copy. No one bought it. Crane had been prepared for shocked condemnation of *Maggie*, but it had not occurred to him that the book might be ignored. He said later, "I remember how I looked forward to its publication, and pictured the sensation I thought it would make. It fell flat. Nobody seemed to notice it or care for it . . . Poor Maggie! she was one of my first loves."

He sent a copy to Hamlin Garland with the inscription:

> It is inevitable that you will be greatly shocked by the book but continue please with all possible courage to the end. For it tries to show that environment is a tremendous thing in the world and frequently shapes lives regardless. If one proves that theory one makes room in Heaven for all sorts of souls (notably an occasional street girl) . . . not confidently expected to be there by many excellent people.

In making this observation about the environment's role in the forming of human character, Crane was stating a major belief that formed his own outlook on life and embracing a literary theory called naturalism, which argued that one's environment was the determinant factor in a person's life and character. *Maggie: A Girl of the Streets* went far beyond the literary theories of Hamlin and Howells. It would ultimately be called America's first naturalistic novel.

To celebrate the book's publication, the Pendennis Club threw a party. Guests were greeted at the door with copies of *Maggie*. "Mustard-yellow piles" of books filled every available space. Punch was poured, and the success of *Maggie* toasted many times over. Stephen strummed his banjo, and the singing became so loud that the landlady climbed the stairs and screamed at them to be quiet. Crane talked to her through a crack in the door, frantically signaling behind his back for the group to be quiet. "The animals apologize and will return to their cages," he promised the landlady. Closing the door, he told his friends, "Cheese it . . .! She'll throw me out . . . We owe her a month's rent as it is."

Throughout March and April, Crane spent long hours at Linson's studio reading old issues of *Century Magazine*. The magazine had run a series called "Battles and Leaders of the Civil War," which included graphic accounts of various battles and the recollections of soldiers who fought in them.

One day, Linson was painting and Stephen was "squatting like an Indian among the magazines," when he suddenly threw one down in disgust and stood up. "I wonder," he fumed, "that *some* of these fellows don't tell how they *felt* in those scraps. They spout eternally of what they *did*, but they are as emotionless as rocks!" Nonetheless, these accounts planted the seeds that would blossom into *The Red Badge of Courage* a year later.

Near the end of March, Crane sent a copy of *Maggie* to William Dean Howells. Stephen was so eager to hear the great critic's opinion that he waited only a week before writing a follow-up letter. "Having recieved [sic] no reply [must I] decide then that you think it a wretched thing?"

Howells immediately responded that he had not yet had time to read the book. But he added, "From the glance I was able to give it, I thought you were working in the right way."

A few weeks later, Howells invited Crane to tea at his house. Stephen borrowed a suit from a friend for the occasion. Howells praised *Maggie* during this visit, but what pleased Stephen most was that Howells introduced him to Emily Dickinson's poetry, reading aloud to him from a recently published volume. The poems made a dramatic and lasting impression on Crane. He had never seriously considered writing poetry, but hearing Dickinson's innovative verse would change that.

Stephen had never forgotten Lily Brandon Monroe, and shortly after his visit with Howells, he wrote to her. "Well, at least I've done something. I wrote a book . . . The book has made me a powerful friend in W.D. Howells." Still confident at this time that *Maggie* would eventually sell, he boasted, "So I think I can say that . . . I'm almost a success. And 'such a boy, too,' they say."

The Pendennis Club disbanded in late April, and Stephen again went to live with his brother Edmund in Lake View. The Civil War novel that had been forming in his mind had now reached fruition. He knew the story he wanted to write, and he knew the main character through and through. He felt ready to write the book. At Edmund's there would be few distractions and the unusual luxury of enjoying three meals a day.

Chapter Five

The Red and the Black

Throughout the summer of 1893, Stephen worked on the war novel, which he initially titled *Private Fleming, His various battles*. He wrote at night after Edmund and his family had gone to bed. If the writing went well, he worked late into the night. He usually slept until noon and ate his breakfast with Edmund's wife and children while they had lunch. He played football in the afternoon with the neighborhood children.

"As soon as the story began to take shape," Edmund recalled, "he read it to me . . . He told me he did not want my literary opinion, only to know if I liked the story . . . He had the confidence of genius."

In the latter part of September, after completing several drafts of the novel, Stephen moved back to New York. He settled into an old building on East Twenty-third Street, where he shared a large studio with three artists. Frederick Gordon, an artist who occupied a studio in the same building, later recalled: "The upper floors were filled with artists, musicians and writers, young men and women, decent people all, who were glad of the low rents and really congenial atmosphere."

This bohemian environment clearly proved stimulating for Stephen. Between the fall of 1893 and spring of 1894, he worked at a frenetic pace: writing short pieces for newspapers and magazines, completing a final draft of the war novel, beginning a new novel called *George's Mother*, and composing poems for a book of poetry.

During this period, he continued to write agonizing love letters to Lily Monroe. "It is beyond me to free myself . . . from my love for you," he wrote. "It comes always between me and what I would enjoy in life . . . [But] it is better to have known you and suffered, than never to have known you."

There is no doubt that Stephen was crushed by Lily's rejection, but his emotional letters suggest that part of the attraction was due to his own quirky personality: He seemed drawn to whatever was unattainable or presented a challenge.

In February 1894, a blizzard hit New York City, dropping almost a foot and a half of snow. Icy winds that reached up to forty miles an hour whipped through the city. While this blizzard raged, Stephen spent most of one night shivering in the Bowery in order to research an article on the homeless.

The following day, his friend Linson found him "looking haggard and almost ill." Stephen had braved the freezing wind and cold, dressed only in rags, in order to observe the homeless men. When Linson asked him why he did not at least wear two or three undershirts beneath the rags, Stephen responded, "How would I know how those poor devils felt if I was warm myself?" Then he showed Linson a hand-written manuscript titled "The Men in the Storm," which he had written as soon as he returned home.

Stephen's literary gurus, Garland and Howells, knew that he always needed money. In early March, they wrangled an assignment for him with the Bacheller and Johnson newspaper syndicate to write about the Bowery's cheap rooming houses—commonly called flophouses. Crane invited one of his roommates, William Carroll, to accompany him on a fact-finding mission.

"We went as hoboes," Carroll recalled, "with about thirty cents each, endured much misery for four days and three nights, and landed finally at Corwin Knapp Linson's studio." Drawing on this experience, Crane wrote a powerful sketch that vividly depicted the despair that engulfed the slums.

However, Crane was not writing solely for newspapers. In mid-March, he went to Hamlin Garland's home to show Garland some of his recently composed "lines." (Stephen always referred to his poems as lines.) Garland read them with "delight and amazement." When he asked if there were any more, Stephen pointed to his forehead and said: "I've got five or six all in a little row up here. That's the way they come—in little rows, all made up, ready to be put down on paper."

Garland, who was interested in psychic phenomenon, especially automatic handwriting, accepted this without question. Stephen apparently saw no need to point out that his "lines"—whether or not they came from the spirit world—often needed revising.

Garland urged Stephen to show the poems to Howells. He did, but Howells was less impressed. He recognized that they were the work of a creative mind, but he disliked poetry that did not rhyme. He pronounced the poems as being "too orphic [mystic]" for his taste. Nevertheless, Howells tried to interest the publisher of *Harper's* in them. When *Harper's* would not publish them, Howells wrote to Crane, "I wish you had given them more form, for then things so striking would have found a public ready made for them; as it is they will have to make one."

Stephen, undeterred, showed the poems to John D. Barry, an editor who had published some of Garland's work. Barry, according to Garland, "fired them off to Copeland and Day," a progressive publishing house known for taking chances on new, avant-garde writers.

Meanwhile, Crane had continued to revise his war novel. In April 1894, he showed part of the manuscript to Garland. Thirty years later, Garland would still remember how much the work impressed him. "I daren't tell you," he told Stephen at the time, "how much I value this thing." When he asked where the rest of the manuscript was, Stephen confessed that it was "in hock" with a typist. He owed the typist fifteen dollars, which he did not have. Garland arranged to loan him the money and asked to see the second half of the novel as soon as possible.

Once Garland had the full manuscript, he did some editing, making penciled corrections and word substitutions on certain pages. He also cautioned Crane against using too much dialect. Stephen did not resent Garland's advice. On the contrary, he carefully considered all of his suggestions, accepting some, rejecting others.

By the end of April, Stephen had completed a final revision. At that time, he changed the title to *The Red Badge of Courage, An Episode of the Civil War*.

He first offered the novel to Samuel S. McClure, who headed the McClure Features Syndicate and also published *McClure's Magazine*. McClure wanted to publish the book, but he was in financial trouble. The stock market had crashed just a year earlier, and money was still tight. It was not a good time to take a chance on an unknown author.

McClure stalled, hoping to keep the novel in his hands until the economy improved. Telling Stephen that he was considering the novel for publication, McClure offered him an interim assignment to explore the working conditions of a Scranton, Pennsylvania, coal mine. He hired Linson to accompany Crane and supply the illustrations.

The two friends went to Scranton in May. Twice Stephen descended into the mine—an experience he did not relish—before writing the article, "In the Depths of a Coal Mine." It was published in McClure's syndicated newspapers and featured in *McClure's Magazine*. Much to Crane's disgust, however, McClure cut the parts that were "overly critical of business interests."

Crane initially submitted his manuscript *The Red Badge of Courage* to S.S. McClure.
(Courtesy of the University of Virginia)

"The birds didn't want the truth after all," Crane told Linson. "Why the hell did they send me up there then? Do they want the public to think the coal mines [are] gilded ball-rooms with the miners eating ice-cream in [spotless] shirt-fronts?"

June found Stephen in Port Jervis, still waiting to hear from McClure about *The Red Badge of Courage.* Throughout the summer, Stephen alternated living with his brothers William and Wilbur in Port Jervis, and with Edmund, who had now moved to a house in Hartwood, New York. Edmund's house became the closest thing to a home that Crane would have in America. Hartwood, which was near Port Jervis, became his favorite retreat when he needed to get out of the city.

In August, Stephen went on a month-long camping trip arranged by Frederic Lawrence's friends and relatives to celebrate Lawrence's graduation from medical school. Linson remembered that "Stephen was [as] happy there as a colt let loose in pasture. The freedom of the woods and the youthful horseplay of the land and water sports were good medicine . . . In the orange light of a great campfire we gathered of evenings and perched on . . . logs, Stephen with his back to a tree picking at a guitar."

Nevertheless, even in this carefree atmosphere, Stephen could not help wondering about the fate of his novel, still held by McClure. Also, Copeland and Day had not yet made a definite commitment to publish his "lines."

On August 23, he wrote a terse note to Copeland and

Day from the campsite. "I would like to hear from you concerning my poetry . . . I have not heard from you in some time. I am in the dark in regard to your intentions."

The camping trip ended in September, and Stephen returned to Hartwood where he worked and played—both with equal intensity. As an acquaintance noted, "Stephen was a furious loafer, a furious worker, a furious smoker, and a furious arguer."

He was always up for a baseball game, or for a croquet match with the young women who frequented Hartwood. But playing with his nieces and nephews gave him special joy. William's daughter Edna never forgot the fun and laughter of those days. She described those times with her uncle:

> We children would have remembered Uncle Stephen if he had never written a word, for we never had a more charming playmate. Whole mornings he spent chasing us around, we a band of law breakers, he a 'red-headed police-man' . . . He was so entirely one of us that when someone told me that he had written a book that was making him famous, I had to laugh. Uncle Stephen famous? It was a joke.

The trees around Hartwood had begun turning from green to gold by the time Copeland and Day agreed to publish Crane's poems. However, the firm rejected some of the more controversial ones, and asked that Stephen write new ones to replace them. Angered by this, Stephen responded: "It seems to me that you cut all the ethical sense out of the book. All the anarchy, perhaps. [And] it is the anarchy which I particularly insist upon. From the poems which you keep you could produce what might be termed a 'nice little volume of verse by Stephen Crane,' but for me there would be no satisfaction."

Unfortunately, as an almost unknown writer, Stephen was in no position to insist on his own way. He apparently recognized this because when he returned to New York City on September 27, he wrote Copeland and Day and accepted the proffered royalty of ten percent. He asked that the poems be untitled and suggested the book be called *The Black Riders and Other Lines*. The publisher voiced no objections and signed the contract.

Slowly, but steadily, a handful of critics and editors began to recognize and acknowledge Stephen's talent. In October, *Arena* magazine published "The Men in the Storm," his story about the Bowery during the blizzard. The editor wrote in the same issue: "Mr. Stephen Crane's little story is a powerful bit of literature. This young writer belonging to the new school [of writing] is likely to achieve in his own field something like the success Hamlin Garland has attained in his."

By the middle of October, perhaps encouraged by his recently signed book contract, Crane had had enough of McClure's stalling. He took *The Red Badge of Courage* to Edward Marshall, the Sunday editor of the *New York Press*. Marshall suggested that he show it to Irving Bacheller, who might syndicate the novel—that is, serialize it in multiple newspapers.

According to Bacheller, Crane handed him a bundle

of paper and said: "Mr. Howells and Hamlin Garland have read this stuff and they think it's good. I wish you'd read it and whether you wish to use the story or not, I'd be glad to have your frank opinion of it." Bacheller took it home with him that evening, and he never forgot reading *The Red Badge of Courage* for the first time: "My wife and I spent more than half the night reading it aloud to each other . . . In the morning I sent for Crane and made an arrangement with him to use about fifty thousand of his magic words as a serial."

Stephen wrote to Garland, who had been in Chicago since April: "I can [now] write you a letter that wont [sic] make you ill. McClure was a Beast about the war-novel . . . He kept it for six months until I was near mad . . . Finally, I took it to Bacheller's. They use it in January."

In late November, Stephen borrowed fifteen dollars from a friend to pay for a revised, condensed typescript of *The Red Badge of Courage*. The Bacheller syndicate ran the much-shortened version of the book in early December, first in the *Philadelphia Press* over three days, and then in a single issue of the *New York Press*. The novel eventually appeared in 750 newspapers across the country. "Somebody has written clean from California about The Red Badge," Crane wrote gleefully.

Around December 17, Crane took two of his short newspaper sketches as examples of his work to the office of Ripley Hitchcock. Hitchcock was a literary advisor to Appleton and Company, a publishing firm. After reading the sketches, he asked Stephen if he had a story long enough for a book. Stephen told him he had written "one rather long story, which was appearing in a Philadelphia newspaper." Hitchcock asked him to send copies immediately. Crane forwarded the newspaper clippings of *The Red Badge of Courage*. As soon as Hitchcock read the story, he assured Stephen that Appleton would publish it in book form.

Eighteen ninety-four had ended in triumph for Crane. Although it had been a roller coaster year with ups and down, highs and lows, Crane had been unbelievably creative and productive.

"I have just crawled out of the fifty-third ditch into which I have been cast," Stephen wrote Hamlin Garland. On December 7, 1894, the *Philadelphia Press* proclaimed, "Stephen Crane is a new name now and unknown, but everybody will be talking about him if he goes on as he has begun."

After the struggling, starving, uncertain years, Stephen was on his way. At twenty-three years old, time seemed to stretch out before him in an endless ribbon of days and years.

Chapter Six

New Horizons

The following year began in a flurry of activity. Irving Bacheller—eager to capitalize on his successful syndication of *The Red Badge of Courage*—offered Crane an assignment to travel throughout the West and Mexico as a sort of roving reporter. Stephen, who had long talked of going west, was quick to accept.

Meanwhile, Copeland and Day was preparing *Black Riders and Other Lines* for publication. This would be the first book published under Stephen's own name, and he was eager to see it in print. Scheduled to leave at the end of January, he scrambled to provide the publisher with a dedication, corrected proofs, and answers to questions about the artwork. By January 28, however, *Black Riders* was still not ready.

Other unfinished business also remained. Stephen had not received the promised contract from Appleton to publish *Red Badge of Courage* in book form. Nevertheless, he could delay his trip for Bacheller no longer.

Leaving a forwarding address, he boarded a train headed west.

He stopped briefly in Philadelphia and St. Louis, but his ultimate destination was Nebraska. That state, hit by severe drought the previous summer, was now being battered by fierce winter storms. Farmers were suffering from shortages of food, shelter, and clothing, and Nebraska's distressing situation had become a national concern.

Stephen stopped first at the *Nebraska State Journal's* office in Lincoln, where he was introduced to Willa Cather, an aspiring writer two years younger than he. "This was the first man of letters I had ever met in the flesh," Cather later wrote, "and when the young man announced who he was, I dropped into a chair behind the editor's desk where I could stare at him." She described Crane as a thin, bedraggled young man:

> He was thin to emaciation . . . His face was gaunt and unshaven, a thin dark moustache straggled on his upper lip, his . . . hair grew low on his forehead and was shaggy and unkempt . . . He wore a flannel shirt and a slovenly apology for a necktie, and his shoes were dusty and worn . . . His eyes [were] the finest I have ever seen . . . full of lustre and changing lights . . . eyes that seemed to be burning themselves out.

Crane soon left Lincoln and traveled deeper into the drought area to interview the struggling farmers. He was caught in a blizzard that gave him a small taste of what the farmers faced. "The thermometer . . . registers eighteen degrees below zero," he wrote. "[And] the temperature of [my] room . . . is precisely one and a half degrees below zero."

After four or five days and some two hundred miles, Crane returned to Lincoln to interview various government officials. In and out of the *Journal* office, he often encountered Willa Cather, who hung about hoping to talk to him about his writing. However, he ducked all her attempts to draw him into a serious conversation.

"[He] was moody most of the time; his health was bad and he seemed profoundly discouraged," Cather later wrote. Then on his last night in Lincoln he began to talk to Cather. He told her that he "led a double literary life; writing . . . first [what] pleased himself, and doing it very slowly; [then writing] any sort of stuff that would sell."

"The detail of a thing has to filter through my blood," he said, "and then it comes out like a native product, but it takes forever." This may have accounted for the discouraged attitude noted by Cather, because during this journey he had no time to let ideas "filter." He had to write quickly, then forward the articles to Bacheller before moving on to another place. Nevertheless, he wrote his Nebraska story in beautiful, poetic prose that stressed the "steadfast and unyielding courage" of the people. Titled "Nebraska's Bitter Fight for Life," it was the best piece he would write on the entire tour.

On February 14, Crane left Nebraska and headed south, making stops at Hot Springs, Arkansas; New

Orleans, Louisiana; and San Antonio, Texas. Along the way he dispatched articles to Bacheller, among them pieces on the Mardi Gras celebration in New Orleans and the Alamo in San Antonio. In between articles, he worked on *The Red Badge of Courage*, restoring the text that had been cut to shorten it for newspaper syndication. In the process, he added a new last sentence: "Over the river a golden ray of sun came through the hosts of leaden rain clouds."

The night before he left San Antonio for Mexico, Stephen wrote a letter to a friend, revealing both fatigue and frustration, "I would tell you of many strange things I have seen," he wrote, "if I was not so bored with writing of them in various articles."

Mexico, however, fired his imagination. He observed and described everything: street vendors, boatmen piloting their crafts along the Viga Canal, and "Indian girls with bare brown arms" selling hat bands made of flowers to the caballeros. Always affected by color, his Mexican stories are awash with the shades and hues of Mexico—"crimson, purple, orange, tremendous colors that, in the changes of the sunset, manoeuvred in the sky like armies."

He tried to write about the poor in Mexico, but found he could not. "The most worthless literature of the world," he said, "has been that written by the men of one nation concerning the men of another."

However, Mexico offered him the real-life adventure he always seemed to crave. He hired a small, speedy horse and a guide, and together they rode out into the

Mexican desert. One night, when they were asleep in a home that offered bed and board, a group of Mexican bandits burst into the room, threatening to kill Stephen if he did not hand over his money and possessions.

Luckily, the bandits were momentarily distracted, and Stephen and his guide managed to escape. They mounted their horses and galloped off across the desert. But the bandits soon followed in hot pursuit. Just as they were about to overtake the two fleeing men, a patrol of Mexican police on horseback appeared and saved the day.

Stephen would turn this unnerving encounter into a short story titled "One Dash—Horses." The hero of his story—not surprising, given Crane's love for horses—was the swift little horse.

In May, Stephen returned to New York. He had been in Mexico so long that his face had turned "the color of a brick side-walk." His journey had been grueling, stimulating, and sometimes frustrating, but it provided him with new subjects and settings. Two of his best short stories, "The Blue Hotel" and "The Bride Comes to Yellow Sky," resulted from this trip.

Only three days before he arrived back in New York, *The Black Riders and Other Lines* appeared in print. The book was laid out just as Stephen had requested, with the poems printed entirely in capital letters, one poem to a page, all untitled. The book's design drew almost as much attention as the poems. The *Chicago Daily Inter-Ocean* sarcastically commented: "The most remarkable thing about this neatly printed little volume

[*Black Riders*] is the amount of blank paper . . . But after reading, you may well be glad that it is so. There is not a line of poetry from the opening to the closing page."

Stephen returned to the old Art Students' Building with a tan, a serape, colorful tales, and, as his friends quickly discovered, no money. Resuming his usual work habits, he wrote at night and "got by largely on a diet of coffee and cigars." This unhealthy lifestyle, combined with his persistent hacking cough, worried his friends.

"We fellows thought Crane's constant smoking, too much coffee, lack of food and poor teeth—at 23— would soon kill him off," said Nelson Green, with whom Crane shared a room. "We told him so and tried to make him go to a dentist. He had the worst teeth I ever saw on a human being—but he would do nothing about it."

Stephen had been back only a short time when professional reviews of *Black Riders* began appearing. A highly respected reviewer for the *Bookman* praised Crane as "a bold—sometimes too bold—original, and powerful writer of eccentric verse." However, most reviewers were not as kind. The *New York Tribune*, continuing to exhibit deep hostility toward its former correspondent, dismissed the book as "so much trash."

However, Stephen was gaining recognition among editors and other writers. In mid-May, he was invited to join the Lantern Club, a new literary society organized by a group of young writers and journalists. A shanty built atop the roof of an old house near the Brooklyn Bridge served as the club's headquarters. Irving Bacheller, the club's president, described the club's meetings: "At our dinners we read short tales and poems to one another . . . We were no mutual-admiration society. It was hard to get a word of praise from any of us." One member, Willis Hawkins, became Stephen's close friend.

Meanwhile in June, the first issue of a new monthly magazine appeared. Titled *Philistine: A Periodical of Protest*, it was a brazen, satirical publication meant to offer an alternative to the more staid magazines of the day. The editor, Elbert Hubbard, was eager to publish edgy writers such as Stephen Crane.

He sent Stephen a complimentary copy of the magazine and asked him to contribute poetry. In this initial publication, Hubbard reviewed *The Black Riders* and reprinted one of its poems, "I saw a man pursuing the horizon." In the next issue, he parodied that poem: "I saw a man making a fool of himself;/He was writing a poem." Anxious for Stephen to submit his work, Hubbard implored him not to take this parody to heart because "we will take it all back in [the] next issue . . . We will try awfully hard to help you," he promised. "You are the coming man I believe."

Unruffled by the parody, Crane responded by sending the *Philistine* two new poems. The fledgling magazine was not yet making enough money to pay contributing authors, but Hubbard promised to run a full-page advertisement for *The Red Badge of Courage* if Crane would donate the poems. Stephen agreed. Throughout Stephen's lifetime, Hubbard would provide a steady market for his poetry.

On June 17, 1895, Crane signed a contract with D.

Appleton and Company to publish *The Red Badge of Courage*. The terms were not good, but Stephen, eager to have the book published, agreed to them.

He joined his friends in August for their annual campout. "I am cruising around the woods in corduroys and feeling great," he wrote Willis Hawkins from camp. "There are six girls in camp and it is with the greatest difficulty that I think coherently on any other subject." It was fortunate that he enjoyed this summer respite because his life would never again be so simple.

In late September, *The Red Badge of Courage* appeared in print, priced at one dollar. Magazines and newspapers began running reviews of the book almost immediately. They came first in dribbles, then in torrents.

The *New York Press* rhapsodized over the novel's vivid descriptions and its realism. The *New York Times* called it "a picture which seems to be extraordinarily true, free from any suspicion of ideality." The *Chicago Post* deemed it "splendid and all aglow with color, movement, and vim," and the *Boston Times* said it was "the most realistic and ghastly picture of the late war which has ever come to our attention."

Stephen, more accustomed to ridicule than praise, retreated to Edmund's house. From there he continued to submit poems to the *Philistine* and send short stories to other publications. He also started another novel which he titled *The Third Violet*.

In November, he received a formal invitation from Elbert Hubbard. "Recognizing . . . your genius as a poet

. . . The Society of the Philistines desire to give a dinner in your honor." Crane immediately wrote to his friend Hawkins, imploring, "Write me at once and tell me how to get out of the thing."

Despite his initial panic, however, Stephen admitted later that he was also overwhelmed by feelings of "pride and arrogance to think that I have such friends." Hawkins encouraged him to attend, even promising to loan him the proper clothes to wear. Although he still harbored doubts, Stephen finally accepted the invitation. His family's reaction may have influenced his decision. He told Hawkins: "You ought to see the effect of such things upon my family . . . It's great. I am no longer a black sheep but a star."

After receiving Crane's acceptance, Hubbard responded, "You represent a 'cause' and we wish in a dignified . . . elegant manner to recognize that cause." The event, however, held on December 19, turned out to be anything but dignified. It was more of a rowdy roast of Crane than a tribute.

Despite the somewhat ribald nature of the gathering, Stephen would always perceive the *Philistine* dinner as an honor, shrugging off the gibes and insults made at his expense. After the banquet ended, Hubbard invited him to his home where they spent several happy, carefree days horseback riding.

Meanwhile, Appleton had sold the British publication rights to *The Red Badge of Courage*—without Crane's knowledge, and without arranging for a royalty to be paid. About a month later, Stephen received a warm and gracious letter from the Heinemann Publishing Company, the English firm that had bought the rights:

> We think so highly of your work—of its . . . literary distinction that we have been very pleased to take special pains to place it prominently before the British public. I have sent about one hundred gratis copies to the leading literary men in this country . . . I think there is no doubt the book will obtain the success it so eminently deserves, & I . . . write to you to say how pleased we are to be identified with your work.

This discerning letter recognizing the value of his work moved Stephen deeply. He desperately needed such confirmation, now more than ever.

As reviewers continued to praise him, he put the finishing touches on *The Third Violet* and sent it to Appleton. However, he had little confidence in the novel. "It's pretty rotten work," he wrote a friend. "I used myself up on the accursed 'Red Badge.' "

Stephen, experiencing his first taste of fame, shivered in the hot winds of success that suddenly whipped around him. The fear that he could never live up to what he had accomplished in *The Red Badge of Courage* haunted him.

Chapter Seven

"I Am, Mostly, Afraid"

By January 1896, Stephen Crane had achieved fame both at home and abroad. In England, where American novels were usually ignored, readers and critics alike showered *The Red Badge of Courage* with extravagant praise. At home, Civil War veterans found his battle descriptions so realistic that some insisted they had fought alongside him—a tribute to Crane's vivid imagination because he had never experienced combat.

In the limelight of his sudden fame, Stephen struggled to maintain a sense of balance. He fled the tumult of New York City and retreated to Edmund's house. From there, on January 27, he wrote to William Dean Howells: "I am slightly rattled and think it best to cling to Hartwood where if I choose to shout triumphant shouts none can hear me. However I have not yet elected to shout . . . I am, mostly, afraid. Afraid that . . . [I will be diverted] from what I believe to be the pursuit of truth . . . If they [critics] would only continue the abuse, I feel [able] to cope with that."

He expressed the same sentiment in a letter to Hitchcock at the Appleton publishing house: "I had grown used to being called a damned ass but this sudden new admiration . . . has made a gibbering idiot of me. I shall stick to my hills."

Floundering in this sea of change, Stephen searched for something or someone to help him stay afloat. Nellie Crouse came to mind. He had met her only once before leaving on his western trip. Now, almost a year later, he wrote her a letter. "You have been for me a curiously potential attraction," he professed. "I don't know what it is or why it is. I have never analyzed it."

It is understandable that he used the word "curiously," because Nellie Crouse, a prim and proper young lady from the Midwest, was not the type of woman who usually captivated Stephen. None of her letters to him have survived, making it difficult to determine if she felt the same attraction. His letters to her indicate that she was enjoying the flirtation, albeit from a safe distance. When he asked for her photo, she sent it without hesitation.

In his letters, Stephen spoke of visiting her in Ohio. He also encouraged her to visit New York, but this was mostly idle talk. Although he was attracted to Nellie's beauty and aloofness, their correspondence served a purpose beyond a romantic dalliance. Stephen needed someone he could pour out his feelings to—someone outside his intimate circle of friends.

In one letter he confessed his greatest fear: "At my publishers yesterday I read long [reviews of *The Red*

Crane sent love letters to Nellie Crouse in 1896.
(Courtesy of Syracuse University)

Badge of Courage] . . . I got an armful of letters from people [about] The Black Riders . . . and then for the first time in my life I began to be afraid, afraid that I would grow content with myself, afraid that . . . I would be satisfied with the little things I have done."

Success laid bare Stephen's vulnerability. His tough guy facade was hard to sustain in the spotlight. The fear that he could never write anything to top *The Red Badge of Courage* continued to stalk him. This was evident in a letter to Hitchcock about *The Third Violet*, "I think it is as well to go ahead with [publishing] The Third Violet," he wrote. "People may just as well discover now that the high dramatic key of The Red Badge cannot be sustained."

Publishers were eager to ride the wave of Crane's success. In February, he wrote Nellie: "I am engaged in [contending] with people who wish me to write more war-stories. Hang all war stories." Nevertheless, he completed a Civil War short story—what he called a "novelette"—titled "The Little Regiment," for *McClure's Magazine*.

Writing the piece was a struggle. "It is awfully hard," he complained to his friend Willis Hawkins. "I have invented the sum of my invention in regard to war and this story keeps me in internal despair." He wrote apologetically to Sam McClure, "I feel for you when I think of some of the things of mine which you will have to read."

In the end, however, he was satisfied with "The Little Regiment." Despite continued protests that he had no more to say about war, he wrote four more war stories.

McClure published only "The Little Regiment" and one other. Later in the year, Appleton would publish all five in a book titled *The Little Regiment and Other Stories.*

In March, Stephen began editing *Maggie*, which Appleton wanted to republish. That same month, he wrote Nellie Crouse to tell her that after spending a few days in New York, he had returned to Hartwood in despair. "It is not that people want to meet me," he wrote. "I can endure [that]. But . . . [my] own friends feel bitterly insulted if I do not see them twelve times a day—in short they are all prepared to find me grown vain . . . That disgraceful Red Badge is doing so very well that my importance has widened and everybody . . . calmly waits to see *me be a chump.*"

This was his last letter to Nellie, who had told him she planned to be married. Sounding every bit the rejected lover, Crane wrote at the end of the letter, "If there is a joy of living I cant [sic] find it." However, in reality, he exhibited little indication of heartbreak. As for Nellie, she knew that Stephen's bohemian ways were more than she cared to handle. Nonetheless, she saved his letters and later boasted to her children that Stephen Crane had once been "deeply in love with her."

At this point, publishers in both America and England clamored for Crane's work. Over the next few months, he sold more than twenty articles to the Bacheller and McClure syndicates. An article about opium users, titled "Opium's Varied Dreams," added fuel to the already circulating false rumors that he was a drug addict and a heavy drinker.

Meanwhile, Crane finished editing *Maggie* for republication. This mostly meant removing words the publisher found offensive—words that would not raise an eyebrow in publishing today. He wrote Hitchcock at Appleton, "I have dispensed with a goodly number of damns."

When summer arrived, Stephen eagerly headed for Hartwood. He had a new saddle horse named Peanuts that he loved—perhaps because the horse acted as unpredictably as he did. Peanuts would sometimes stop in mid-trot if he spotted a small stick in the road, then gather all four legs together and jump the stick as though it were a huge boulder. Stephen and Edmund spent happy summer days recklessly racing their horses along Hartwood's country roads.

Stephen also made time for work. By fall of 1896, he had three novels in print: *George's Mother*, *The Red Badge of Courage*, and *Maggie: A Girl of the Streets*. Arrangements had also been made for publishing *The Third Violet* and *The Little Regiment*. It was the one and only time in Stephen's life that he ever had sufficient money. Life was good.

In September, he agreed to write a series of feature articles for the *New York Journal* on a corrupt, vice-ridden district of New York City called the Tenderloin. Although there were some legitimate theaters, restaurants, and hotels in the Tenderloin, it was most noted for its opium joints, gambling houses, prostitutes, and crooked policemen.

In carrying out this assignment, Stephen incurred

the wrath of the entire New York City Police department. It all began at two o'clock in the morning on September 16, 1896. According to Stephen, he was walking in the Tenderloin with two chorus girls while interviewing them for an article. A prostitute named Dora Clark joined them, and they all walked together to the corner of Broadway and Thirty-first Street. Dora and one of the women waited while Stephen escorted the other one across the street to a cable car. When he returned to the waiting women, a policeman in civilian clothes was arresting Dora Clark for prostitution. Stephen protested that Dora had not been soliciting. He insisted that she had been "perfectly respectable" in the brief time she walked with him and the chorus girls.

When the officer arrested Dora anyway, Stephen followed them to the station house and told the desk sergeant his version of what happened. The sergeant admitted that the officer might have been mistaken in this particular instance, but that he himself knew the girl was a common prostitute. He advised Stephen against getting involved. "If you monkey with this case," he warned, "you are pretty sure to come out with mud all over you."

Nevertheless, Stephen showed up the next morning to testify on Dora Clark's behalf. He waited all morning until finally Dora was brought in. The arresting officer, whose name was Charles Becker, testified that she was "an old offender." When the judge appeared ready to rule against Dora, Stephen intervened.

"Your Honor, I know this girl to be innocent," he

said. "I am the man who was with her, and there is no truth in what the officer has charged." The judge asked for his name, and he responded, "I am Stephen Crane, the novelist." After hearing Stephen's story, the judge released Dora Clark from custody.

The newspapers had a field day, first in New York and then across the country. Their reports focused on Crane rather than on possible police corruption. At first the stories were flattering. "He wore No Red Badge of Courage, But Pluckily Saved a Girl from the Law," one headline read. "Brave as His Hero," read another.

Then the tide turned. The *Chicago Dispatch* noted, "Stephen Crane is respectfully informed that association with women in scarlet is not necessarily a 'Red Badge of Courage.' " Other newspapers also expressed moral disapproval. Stephen, meanwhile, wrote about his experience for the *New York Journal* in a piece titled "Adventures of a Novelist."

The excitement would have ended there, soon to be replaced with fresher news, except for Dora Clark. On October 2, she brought charges of harassment and wrongful arrest against Officer Becker. That same day, the *Boston Traveler* accused Stephen of lying about his reasons for being in the Tenderloin the night Dora Clark was arrested. "The chances are that the youthful literary prodigy was on a genuine 'lark,' and . . . invented the tale about searching for book material," the paper charged.

The trial, which began on October 15, became a nightmare for Stephen, whose freewheeling lifestyle made him an easy target. He was grilled endlessly, accused of everything from immoral philandering to opium addiction. What was called "the longest trial ever held at police headquarters" ended at two-thirty in the morning on October 16. Officer Becker was acquitted.

Old friends stood by, but Stephen's life was in shambles, his reputation shattered. He needed to get away from the glare of New York publicity. Fleeing to Hartwood—his usual refuge from trouble—was out of the question, because he did not want to embarrass his brother. Fortunately, Irving Bacheller provided a way out when he again offered Stephen a job as a special correspondent. But this assignment, unlike the earlier one that had sent him to the West and Mexico, would be dangerous.

Bacheller believed that Cuba's recent uprising against Spanish rule would eventually develop into a full-scale revolution. When it did, he wanted a reporter on the scene. This would mark Stephen's first experience as a war correspondent, but not his last. Reporting from the battlefront became a vocation that he followed off and on for the rest of his life.

Stephen left New York for Jacksonville, Florida, en route to Cuba, in November 1896. Bacheller had provided him with a money belt and seven hundred dollars in Spanish gold. Stephen must have breathed a sigh of relief when the train pulled out of the station. Whatever he would face when he reached Havana surely seemed preferable to the hullabaloo of the past few months. He finally had an opportunity to see for himself what real war was like.

Chapter Eight

Adrift

In Jacksonville, Stephen checked into the classy St. James Hotel and began looking for a ship that would take him to Cuba. This was no easy task. First, he was only one of many reporters seeking passage, and second, the secrecy and intrigue that surrounded ships sailing to Cuba made it difficult to get information. Captains were wary of spies because they carried contraband—illegal guns and ammunition—for the Cuban rebels.

Aware of the potential danger he would face, Stephen dictated a will and sent it to his brother William, who was a lawyer. He enclosed a letter assuring William that he had "acted like a man of honor and a gentleman" in the recent Dora Clark matter. (Despite his lifelong indifference to what others thought of him, Stephen never got over wanting to please his brothers.)

The same day he wrote to William, he wrote his friend Willis Hawkins regarding yet another romantic entanglement, "In case you see Amy . . . encourage her in every possible way." He was speaking of former actress Amy Leslie, a well-known drama critic, sixteen years older than Stephen. The two had been romantically linked at the time he left New York, and he wrote her from Florida, "I think of you, night and day, my own love."

For unclear reasons, he had given Hawkins a sum of money to give Amy if she requested it. This eventually led to a misunderstanding, when Amy claimed the money was hers to begin with. In any case, Stephen continued to write her love letters for some time, even after he became involved with someone else.

He spent most of his time in Jacksonville hanging around waterfront saloons, hoping to connect with a ship. One evening, however, he went with some other reporters to the Hotel de Dream—an establishment variously described as a hotel, a nightclub, and a brothel.

An elegant woman named Cora Stewart owned the Hotel de Dream. Energetic and vital, Cora was six years older than Stephen. She had blue eyes and wore her lovely red-gold hair upswept and coiled around her head. She clothed her ample figure in understated clothes and carried herself with a regal air. One of Crane's fellow correspondents recalled years later, "Fact is, she was a cut above us in several ways, notably poise and surety of command of herself and others."

Cora came from a middle-class background, had traveled in Europe, and was well read. Like Stephen, she was a rebel who lived life on her own terms. She had already had two brief, failed marriages. Her second husband was Donald Stewart, the son of a British baronet. They had lived in London after their marriage. She soon left him for someone else, although he refused to grant her a divorce. This did not prevent Cora from falling madly in love with Stephen, which by all accounts happened the first time she met him.

Shortly after meeting Cora, however, Stephen secured passage for Cuba aboard the *Commodore*, a coal-burning tugboat. The ship sailed at 8:00 P.M. on New Year's Eve, carrying sixteen Cuban guerrillas and a crew of eleven men, including Crane.

Trouble ensued from the start. Less than two miles out, the *Commodore* struck a sandbar. It was daybreak before a patrol ship towed the tug free. Unfortunately, Captain Edward Murphy then headed for the open sea without checking for structural damage.

Within hours the ship began to take on water. The pumps failed, and the engine room flooded. Stephen joined the others in a bucket brigade, bailing water and passing the filled pails down the line. All the while rough seas caused the tug to roll and pitch wildly. Bailing water in the oppressive heat of the engine room, the inevitable cigarette dangling from his lips, Stephen removed his new shoes and tossed them overboard. "I guess I won't need them if we have to swim," he told the captain with a laugh.

The struggle to keep the ship afloat continued throughout the night. The captain sent up distress flares, but no help came. Finally, in the early morning hours of January 2, the crew lowered three lifeboats full of men

Crane met Cora Stewart in Jacksonville, Florida, while on his way to cover the revolution in Cuba. *(Courtesy of Syracuse University)*

into the ocean. This left four men on the ship: Captain Murphy, who now had a broken arm, Billy Higgins, the ship's oiler, C.B. Montgomery, the cook, and Stephen Crane. There were no more lifeboats aboard—only a ten-foot dinghy. Having no other choice, the four men jammed into the tiny boat.

Captain Murphy remembered the waves as they pushed away from the foundering *Commodore*: "They rolled in on us, threatening to dash us against the sinking tug, and we expected every moment to be overthrown. It was pitch dark, and you could not see your hands before your face." What followed would remain embedded in Stephen's memory forever.

He watched in horror from the dinghy as one of the three lifeboats capsized. The seven men who had occupied the lifeboat re-boarded the *Commodore* and hastily built and lowered makeshift rafts into the water. One man was killed when he jumped from the ship to one of the rafts. Three refused to jump and went down with the *Commodore*. Two others were lost when the sinking ship sucked their rafts under.

One man still survived, clinging to his raft. He threw a line to the overburdened dinghy that Montgomery caught. Stephen and the oiler rowed frantically in an effort to tow the man's raft away from the sinking tug. It was impossible. When the man began pulling the dinghy toward him, there was nothing to do but drop the line and watch as the whirlpool created by the *Commodore* swallowed up the terrified man. The ship sank at approximately 7:00 A.M.

The men in the remaining two lifeboats would safely reach shore by noon, but Stephen and his companions were not so fortunate. They battled the heavy seas and strong winds all that day and throughout the following night. The large waves threatened to capsize the tiny dinghy at any moment.

Once, they came within a half-mile of the shore, but darkness and heavy surf prevented them from reaching it. "We were afraid to trust ourselves in the seething breakers," the cook later told a *Journal* reporter. "So we laid there where we were all the rest of the night and worked for our lives . . . in the effort to keep our boat from filling." Stephen and Higgins, the oiler, took turns rowing. "A night on the sea in an open boat is a long night," Stephen later wrote.

When morning finally dawned, they could see Daytona Beach, but no people. Despite numbing exhaustion and the continued roughness of the surf, they decided to try landing the dinghy. Almost immediately the little craft overturned, dumping its four passengers into the icy water. The powerful undertow made staying afloat difficult. Fortunately, a man walking along the beach spotted them. "He dashed into the water and grabbed the cook," Crane said later. "Then he went after the captain, but the captain sent him to me, and then it was that we saw Billy Higgins lying with his forehead on sand that was clear of the water, and he was dead."

The three survivors were fed and given medical treatment. Stephen sent off telegrams, including one to Cora. Several newspapers had reported him dead, and Cora was overjoyed to hear he was alive. She telegraphed immediately, "Thank God [you're] safe have been almost crazy." The next day she arrived in Daytona to accompany the exhausted and emotionally drained writer back to Jacksonville by train.

Once again, Stephen made the news, but this time in a positive way. Surviving shipmates spoke of his bravery. Captain Murphy praised his courage in an interview with the *New York Press*. "That man Crane is the spunkiest fellow . . . The sea was so rough that even old sailors got seasick . . . but Crane behaved like a born sailor . . . When the leak was discovered he was the first man to volunteer aid . . . He's a brave man . . . with plenty of grit."

Stephen remained in Jacksonville until he finished writing his own account of the harrowing experience for Bacheller—even though the seven hundred dollars in gold now lay at the bottom of the sea. Then on January 13, he returned to New York. He spent three weeks visiting his brothers and writing a fictionalized version of his recent experience—a longish short story titled "The Open Boat." Recognized today as a literary classic, "The Open Boat" explores a theme that always intrigued Crane: man's futile struggle against a cruel and indifferent universe.

Earlier, in September 1896, he had retained a literary agent named Paul Revere Reynolds. He hoped that Reynolds could help him break into the international magazines that published simultaneously in New York and London. In March 1897, Reynolds sold "The Open Boat" to *Scribner's Magazine* for three hundred dollars.

By then, Crane had returned to Jacksonville with Cora, where he tried once again to get to Cuba. On March 11, he wrote to his brother William, "I have changed all my plans." The *New York Journal* was sending him to cover an impending war between Greece and Turkey.

First, however, he returned briefly to New York City, where he called on Sam McClure. For a personal loan of a mere six hundred dollars, he gave McClure first option on all of his future short stories, as well as the book rights to "The Open Boat." Stephen was broke and desperate for money, but this foolish action would keep him indebted to McClure for much of his remaining life.

Stephen sailed for Liverpool, England, on March 20. From there he would proceed to Crete. Whether he encouraged Cora to come with him, or whether she herself insisted on coming, is unclear. In any event, she followed on a separate ship a few days later.

In London, where *The Red Badge of Courage* had been a huge success, Crane was treated like a celebrity. He met his English publisher, William Heinemann, who welcomed him warmly. Richard Harding Davis, an American journalist and the most famous war correspondent of his generation, held a luncheon in Stephen's honor.

Stephen had arranged with the *New York Journal* for Cora to report the war from a woman's point of view, using the name "Imogene Carter." They first went to Athens. Then, along with a number of other correspondents, they embarked for Thessaly, where heavy Greek losses had been reported. By the time they arrived there, however, the fighting had ended. Although the other reporters continued on to Velestino, Cora and Stephen decided to stay in the quaint mountain village of Volo.

A few days later, the Turks launched a major attack at Velestino. Stephen, twelve miles away at Volo, ill with dysentery and unable to travel, missed the first day of the battle. However, the next day, he and Cora rode to Velestino on horseback, arriving at noon. Here, Stephen finally saw real war for the first time. He was not disappointed.

"The roll of musketry fire . . . was a beautiful sound," he wrote. "It was more impressive than the roar of Niagara and finer than thunder or an avalanche, because it had the wonder of human tragedy in it. It was the most beautiful sound of my experience." In the next paragraph, however, he admitted that the men who died there would have had a different opinion. But the experience had confirmed for him that *The Red Badge of Courage* was, in his words, "all right."

The Greco-Turkish War ended in thirty days. It had consisted mostly of a series of retreats by the Greeks. Despite the brevity of the conflict, however, Stephen sent the *Journal* at least thirteen dispatches. His accounts were never just straight reporting. They always blended literary imagination with actual facts.

Stephen wrote poignantly on watching Greek reserve troops marching up the road under heavy artillery fire: "Reserves coming up passed a wayside shrine.

Stephen and Cora traveled to Greece and Turkey to cover the Greco-Turkish War in 1897. *(Courtesy of Syracuse University)*

There the men paused to cross themselves and pray. A shell struck the shrine and demolished it. The men in the rear of the column were obliged to pray at the spot where the shrine had been."

On May 6, with the Greeks in full retreat from Velestino and the Turks advancing, Cora and Stephen left for Volo. They carried a "fat waddling puppy" that Stephen had rescued on the battlefield and christened "Velestino, the Journal Dog." Stephen wrote a humorous account of the dog in an article for the *Journal* titled "The Dogs of War."

By May 10, the Turks were surrounding Volo, and Stephen and Cora fled to Athens, where Stephen dispatched his report. Ten days later an armistice ended the war, and the two left Athens accompanied by two Greek servants (war refugees) and the dog.

After spending several weeks in Paris, Stephen and Cora decided not to return to America, but to live in England as Mr. and Mrs. Stephen Crane. Such an arrangement would be less frowned upon in England.

Chapter Nine

Exile

Stephen and Cora found a house at Ravensbrook, Oxted Surrey, a few miles outside of London. Although he wrote William that he would be staying in England, Stephen did not mention Cora. He knew that his family would never accept him living unmarried with Cora and that undoubtedly had influenced his decision to remain in England.

That fall and winter he wrote a novella titled *The Monster*. It was set in Wilhomville, a fictional town he modeled on Port Jervis, and may have reflected a longing for home. Two other stories written at that time, "The Bride Comes to Yellow Sky," and "The Blue Hotel," reached back to San Antonio and his western trip.

England's appreciation of his work eased Stephen's homesickness. Critics there were much kinder than in America. Reviewers in London rhapsodized over *The Third Violet*—the same novel Stephen had considered a failure and that American critics were calling inane.

One American critic wrote scathingly that Crane "far from being a great writer, is not even a good writer." But London critics considered him in "the front rank of English and American writers of fiction."

On October 15, 1897—four months after settling at Ravensbrook—Stephen made one of his most gratifying and enduring literary friendships. That day he met Joseph Conrad, whose novel, *The Nigger of the Narcissus*, was then running serially in the *New Review* magazine. The transplanted Polish writer was fourteen years older than Stephen, but the two very different men hit it off from the beginning. On that crisp fall day, they talked and talked, first at a restaurant over a lunch that lasted well into the afternoon, and then while they strolled the streets of London. It was almost midnight when they bid each other goodnight.

The friendship continued to grow through letters and visits. Conrad, who had not been writing as long as Crane, asked Stephen to read the proofs of his novel. "The book is simply great," Stephen wrote him. "The . . . death of Waite is . . . too terrible . . . It caught me very hard. I felt ill over that red thread lining [extending] from the corner of the man's mouth to his chin." The blood coming from Waite's mouth may have reminded Crane of his family's history of lung problems. Tuberculosis often resulted in hemorrhaging.

Meanwhile at Ravensbrook, Stephen and Cora embarked on an extravagant lifestyle that would soon result in an insurmountable mountain of debts. "We have no sense about money at all," Cora once confessed.

Crane became good friends with novelist Joseph Conrad.
(Courtesy of the Library of Congress)

Stephen, attempting to stem the rising tide of debt, flooded his American agent, Paul Reynolds, with articles and stories—some good, some not. He constantly implored Reynolds to secure him larger advances.

Hoping to increase sales, Stephen gave Reynolds full control over any work he published in America. "I will allow you ten percent on the sales and refer everything to you, " he wrote the agent. "One of the reasons . . . is to get me out of the ardent grasp of S.S. McClure Co . . . They seem to calculate on controlling my entire output."

On October 29, Crane wrote William, never directly asking for money, but hinting of financial troubles throughout the letter. "I am just thinking how easy it would be in my present financial extremity to cable you for a hundred dollars but then by the time this reaches you I will probably be all right again."

In December, he sent Reynolds "Death and the Child," his only short story about the Greco-Turkish War. With a desperation that is painful to read, he begged Reynolds, "For heaven's sake raise me all the money you can and *cable* it, *cable* it [for] sure between Xmas and New Year's."

The New Year brought more financial woes when Crane's old lover took him to court. On January 4, 1898, the *New York Times* reported, "Amy Leslie has brought a suit in the Supreme Court [of New York] to recover $550 from Stephen Crane." The lawsuit tied up his royalties from *The Red Badge of Courage*.

Stephen now pushed himself harder than ever. He finished "The Blue Hotel," sent poetry to Elbert Hubbard for publication in the *Philistine*, wrote a table of contents for the English edition of "The Open Boat," and worked on *Active Service*, a novel about the Greek war. He could not produce stories fast enough to keep up with his creditors. In February, after being served with a summons to answer Amy Leslie's claim, he was forced to contact William, who managed to settle the suit out of court.

On February 7, he sent "The Blue Hotel" to Reynolds. "To my mind," Crane wrote, "it is a daisy. If you sell . . .

[it], cable the money instantly . . . Get me through this and I am prepared to smile."

A few days later the *USS Maine* blew up in Havana Harbor, an event that would lead to the Spanish-American war. Stephen paid little attention at the time, but by April, the approaching war in Cuba looked like an opportunity to make some fast money. He was near exhaustion from overwork, and he was restless, weary of the daily grind and the endless stream of creditors knocking on his door.

He scrambled to scrape enough cash together to pay for passage across the Atlantic. On April 13, 1898—just twelve days before the United States declared war on Spain—he sailed aboard the *Germanic* to America. The passenger list described him as "age 26 . . . occupation journalist, citizen of the United States, intended destination New York."

The *New York World* hired Crane to cover the war, reportedly paying him three thousand dollars. By April 26, he had joined a swarm of other reporters in Key West, Florida. For over a month, little happened while the Spanish fleet played tag with the U.S. Navy.

Finally, the Americans blockaded the Spanish fleet, and marines established an American base at Guantanamo Bay on June 10. Stephen, aboard a tug called *The Three Friends*, witnessed their successful landing. That night he did not return to port to cable dispatches, as the other correspondents did, but instead went ashore with the marines.

He spent the night in the trenches with four marine

signalmen who used lanterns to flash messages to American ships in the bay. It was a harrowing night because Spanish soldiers were firing down on them from three directions. Each time a signalman stood to send a message, he presented a perfect target. In a dispatch titled "Marines Signaling Under Fire at Guantanamo," Stephen wrote, "When one of these men stood up to wave his lantern, I, lying in the trench . . . rolled a little to the right or left, in order that, when he was shot, he might not fall on me."

When the other reporters returned, a colleague went looking for Stephen to take him back aboard *The Three Friends*. He found him dirty, disheveled, and red-eyed from exhaustion, sitting on a rock observing the battle—out of the line of fire but close enough to be blanketed with battle smoke. After much persuasion and a promise of cigarettes, Stephen returned to the tug and wrote his report.

Ten days later, Stephen and the other reporters followed Theodore Roosevelt and his Rough Riders as they made their way to Las Guasimas. There, Spanish soldiers ambushed the Americans, and Edward Marshall—a reporter Stephen had known since his days at the Art Students' League in New York—was shot through the spine. Marshall worked for a rival paper, but Stephen volunteered to file his dispatches for him.

Marshall later described what happened:

> When I regained consciousness . . . one of the first faces I saw was that of Stephen Crane. The day was

Crane went to Cuba to cover the Spanish-American War for the *New York World*.
(Courtesy of Syracuse University)

hot . . . something like 100 degrees. Yet Stephen Crane—and mind you, he was there in the interest of a rival newspaper—took the dispatch which I managed to write five or six miles to the coast and cabled it for me. He had to walk, for he could get no horse or mule. Then he . . . arranged with a number of men to bring a stretcher . . . and carry me back on it. He was probably as tired then as a man could be and still walk. But he trudged back . . . to the field hospital . . . and saw to it that I was properly conveyed to the coast.

On July 1, the Rough Riders made their famous charge up San Juan Hill. American casualties were high, and Stephen was shaken when he discovered Reuben McNab lying amidst the fallen soldiers. McNab—an old schoolmate from Claverack College—was badly wounded.

"[He was] identified . . . in my thought with the sunny irresponsible days at Claverack, when all the earth was a green field and all the sky was a rainless blue," Stephen wrote later. "I had looked upon five hundred wounded men with stolidity [unemotionally] . . . but . . . Reuben McNab, the schoolmate, lying there in the mud, with a hole through his lung . . . set me trembling with a sense of terrible intimacy with this war which theretofore I could have believed was a dream—almost."

Shortly after this, Crane collapsed with a high fever from malaria and was put aboard a ship bound for Virginia. He looked so ill that the ship's captain isolated him, suspecting yellow fever. But when the ship docked on July 13, Stephen filed his story on the Battle of San Juan that same afternoon.

He spent the next couple of weeks resting and recuperating. He discarded his torn and filthy clothing, and paid twenty-four dollars for a new suit, which he billed to the *New York World*. Then, at the end of July, he returned to New York and reported in at the *World* office. At that time, his job with the paper ended. He either quit or was fired, it is unclear which. Whatever the case, he immediately signed with the *New York Journal* to report the Puerto Rican campaign—the next and last battle of the Spanish-American War.

He did not visit his family while he was in New York. He did go see Dr. Edward Trudeau, a well-known lung specialist in the Adirondacks. This may not have been the first time Stephen consulted Dr. Trudeau. There is no record of an earlier visit, but a letter from Dr. Trudeau to Cora, written on September 16, 1898, indicated he had previously treated Stephen for lung problems. He may have even made a diagnosis of tuberculosis, because he told Cora, "Your husband had a slight evidence of activity in the trouble in his lungs . . . but it was not serious."

Despite Trudeau's assurance to Cora that Stephen's condition was not serious, Charles Michelson, another *Journal* reporter, thought Crane looked ill. The two reporters sailed together to Puerto Rico shortly after Stephen saw Dr. Trudeau, and Michelson was shocked by his appearance. He described him as "shambling . . . hollow-cheeked, sallow . . . marked with ill-health."

Stephen spent a couple of weeks in Puerto Rico for the *Journal*, but the war was quickly coming to an end. By mid-August, he cabled Cora that he was back in Key West. A week later, he disappeared

Although the Spanish still occupied Cuba and did not welcome American journalists, Stephen somehow slipped into Havana. "I was at a hotel while the Government was . . . imprisoning nine [other] correspondents . . . But no one molested me," Stephen said later. He made no effort to let either Cora, or his family and friends, know his whereabouts. He corresponded only with his agent, Paul Reynolds.

As with so much of Crane's life, it is unclear why he vanished into Havana. Some biographers suggest he was involved with another woman. Others say he was so physically and emotionally exhausted that he could not face returning to England and his mountain of debts. Still, others think he needed time and space to concentrate on writing, hoping to sell enough work to clear his debts. Perhaps he himself had given the answer a year earlier when he told an editor: "I cannot help vanishing and disappearing and dissolving. It is my foremost trait."

In any event, Stephen worked hard in Havana. He sent war story after war story to Reynolds. He wrote innumerable newspaper pieces and worked on his novel *Active Service*. He finished four Cuban war stories to round out a collection of stories for a book called *Wounds in the Rain*. On September 14, he sent the last batch of poems needed for his second book of poetry to be titled *War Is Kind*.

When it was published in April 1899, Crane's book of poetry *War is Kind* received bad reviews. *(Courtesy of the University of Virginia)*

Throughout his stay in Havana, he badgered Reynolds for money. The *Journal* had taken him off the payroll in September for abusing his expense account. Now he actually owed the *Journal* money. In October, Stephen wrote his beleaguered agent: "If I dont [sic] receive a rather fat sum from you before the last of the month, I am *ruined*."

Meanwhile in England, Cora—hounded by creditors and not knowing if Stephen was dead or alive—had turned to the English consul in Havana. When the consul notified her that Stephen was alive, she worried that he might need money to get back to England. Cora had no money to send. She could not even pay the grocer. Finally in desperation, she went through Stephen's papers, found some unpublished stories, and sent them to a young, rapidly rising English agent named James Pinker. When Pinker responded positively, Cora asked him if he would be interested in a book by Stephen. Pinker said yes.

Cora had not heard from Stephen for three months, but by now she had learned of his address in Havana. She wrote to him about Pinker's interest in a book and urged him to come home, assuring him she would not ask any questions. Whatever his reasons for staying away had been, she wanted him back. Either because of Cora's pleading or of the possibility of a book contract with a large advance, Stephen finally left Havana in mid-November.

Even then, he stopped first in New York, where he called on old friends, such as Corwin Knapp Linson and Hamlin Garland. "He strikes me now as he did in early days . . . not a man of long life," Garland wrote in his diary at the time. Again, Stephen did not visit his family, although he must have ached to see them and to ride his beloved horse Peanuts over Hartwood's rolling hills.

On December 31, 1898, he boarded the *Manitou* for England. He had been away from Cora for nine months.

Chapter Ten

The Future Unlived

Stephen arrived back in England on January 11, 1899. Not much had changed. The rent at Ravensbrook had not been paid in a year, and local merchants were clamoring for payment of long overdue bills. Creditors descended on him before he could unpack.

A week after his return, Cora took Stephen to see a house she had discovered while he was away. Brede Place was a sprawling, crumbling, fourteenth-century house situated in the middle of a large park. It had no modern plumbing or electricity, and many of its rooms were in such a state of disrepair that they were unusable. But the history of the house fascinated Stephen, and he liked the idea that the locals thought it was haunted.

Moreton Frewen, an Englishman who liked Americans and enjoyed befriending writers, owned the house. He rented the house to the Cranes for less than half the amount of their yearly rent at Ravensbrook. When he learned they could not move until their back rent was paid, he sent Stephen to his own solicitor, Alfred Plant, for financial advice.

Plant labored to untangle the Crane's messy finances, but he was doomed to fail. Stephen and Cora kept up their extravagant lifestyle, and Stephen, by his own admission, continued to "borrow money from pretty near every body in the world." Nevertheless, Plant's valiant efforts kept them out of bankruptcy and enabled them to move into Brede Place in February.

Despite financial problems and persistent ill health, Stephen was happy with Brede Place. He had room for his three dogs—Sponge, Flannel, and Ruby—and for the first time in a long while, he had a horse to ride. Soon he was happily playing the role of an English squire.

"I hope that the perfect quiet of Brede Place . . . will let him show the world a book that will live," Cora wrote to a friend. However, there was seldom any quiet, perfect or otherwise. A constant flow of visitors streamed through the house, though not all of them were invited. Stephen called these uninvited guests "lice."

"He was beset by people who understood not the quality of his genius," Joseph Conrad wrote. "I don't think he had any illusions about them himself, yet there was a strain of good-nature and perhaps of weakness in his character which prevented him from shaking himself free from their worthless and [patronizing] attentions."

On the other hand, many people came because either

Stephen or Cora invited them. Besides Conrad, other literary people living nearby included Henry James, Ford Maddox Ford, H.G. Wells, and the renowned literary critic Edward Garnett. Stephen enjoyed entertaining them, and he spared no expense.

Perhaps he also needed people around to take his mind off his deteriorating health. Cora called his recurring bouts of illness "Cuban fever," but Stephen probably knew, or at least suspected, that the fevers signaled the worsening of the dreaded consumption, as tuberculosis was then called. At that time, there was no cure for the disease.

Cora had written to William when Stephen was in Havana, therefore he could no longer hide their relationship from his family. Yet he could not bring himself to tell his brother that he and Cora were not legally married. Instead, he lied. "Yes, it is true I am married to an English lady," he wrote, "and . . . we have this beautiful old manor."

Stephen did most of his writing in his study, a small room above the porch. He worked steadily at a desk in front of windows that looked down on the park where he rode his horse. Neither the hotel-like atmosphere at Brede Place nor the symptoms of encroaching tuberculosis kept him from his self-imposed schedule. He moved rapidly from one story to another. He alternately coaxed, bullied, and begged both his agents—Reynolds in America and Pinker in England—to obtain larger advances for him. Cora took over much of his business correspondence so that he could devote more time to writing.

Although he became increasingly sick, Crane kept up his writing pace at Brede Place.
(Courtesy of Syracuse University)

He no longer gave himself the luxury of letting a story mature in his mind before writing it. He wrote, as Conrad's wife said later, "feverishly anxious, too anxious to get the best out of himself." To speed up his output even more, he purchased a typewriter.

In May, Stephen wrote to William boasting about the number of stories he would soon have published. "If you think I am not hustling to get out of this hole you are mistaken," he wrote defensively. However, the next line reveals his desperation. "But sometimes I think I cant [sic] quite do it. Let me know as soon as you see this letter exactly what are the prospects of your lending me five hundred dollars by the first of April."

Around this same time, Stephen wrote to Frewen's wife, Clara, that *Active Service*, the novel begun in Havana, was finished and "being sent forth to the world to undermine whatever reputation for excellence I may have achieved up to this time and may heaven forgive it for being so bad."

War Is Kind, Crane's book of war poems, was published in April to scathing reviews. Reviewer Willa Cather, who had once schemed just to be in the same room with him, wrote: "Either Mr. Crane is insulting the public or . . . he is chattering the primeval nonsense of the apes . . . And [war] is not kind at all, Mr. Crane, when it provokes such verses as these."

Despite his harrowing work schedule, Stephen found time for friends. At least once a week, Henry James bicycled over to Brede Place. In June, the Conrads, who now had a fifteen-month old son, arrived for a two-week visit. Stephen always enjoyed Joseph Conrad's company, and he spent hours playing with his friend's little boy.

Soon after the Conrads left, Stephen acquired an added responsibility when his niece Helen Crane arrived from Port Jervis. William, unhappy with his daughter's behavior, thought she would benefit from attending a European school. He asked Stephen to find

Brede Place became a welcome retreat for the Cranes, and a place where their literary friends would visit.

(Courtesy of Syracuse University)

her a suitable one. She would live at Brede Place until the fall term began.

In mid-July, Stephen decided to make some professional changes. He dropped Reynolds, his long-time American agent, and made Pinker his exclusive agent for both the English and the American market. He never explained why, except to say it was an act of self-preservation.

His health continued to fail, and this caused Cora considerable anxiety. Stephen never wrote or talked much about his feelings for Cora. In August 1899, however, he wrote a letter to an unidentified correspondent that revealed his deep concern.

"Please have the kindness to keep your mouth shut about my health in front of Mrs. Crane hereafter," he wrote. "It is all up with me but I will not have her scared. For some funny woman's reason, she likes me."

As this letter indicates, Stephen knew he probably did not have long to live. He did not want pity. He always had his writing to keep him going. He worked frantically to finish stories for *Wounds in the Rain*. However, even work could not always shut out what was happening to his body.

In September, he wrote to the British undersecretary of state for war: "At present I feel like hell . . . What do you know about the Black Forest [in Germany]? I mean as a health resort? The truth is that Cuba *libre* just about liberated me from this base blue world. The clockwork is juggling badly."

Soon after writing this letter, Stephen took Helen to

Switzerland and enrolled her in school before returning to his desk in Brede Place. He had promised the Frederick A. Stokes Company a novel on the American Revolution, and now he dictated a partial outline of it to Cora. He also finished another Wilholmville story. He called these tales "sure and quick money."

Both Stephen and Cora continually bombarded Pinker for cash advances. The agent had displayed amazing patience, but in October, he rebelled. He wrote to Stephen: "I confess that you are becoming most alarming. You telegraphed on Friday for 20 pounds; Mrs. Crane, on Monday, makes it 50 pounds; today comes your letter making it 150 pounds, and I very much fear that your agent must be a millionaire if he is to satisfy your necessities . . ."

However, Pinker believed in Stephen's talent, and in November, Pinker was rewarded for his faith. Amid all the hack work, the "sure and quick money" kind of writing that Crane had been sending him, a jewel appeared—what Stephen called "a double extra special good thing." The fifteen-hundred-word war story was titled "The Upturned Face." It depicted the burial of a soldier in the Spanish-American War, and "one man's reaction to the face of death." The story had been germinating in Stephen's mind for a long time.

In December, Stephen and Cora threw a lavish Christmas party that lasted three days. The party, suggested by Stephen, had been in the planning since September. They decorated the house with holly and ivy, hired extra servants, rented cots from the local hospital, and engaged an orchestra. The party began on Boxing Day, the day after Christmas.

Many years later, Crane's writer-friend A.E.W. Mason reminisced about the party:

> [Crane] had invited the leading figures of the country-side, but there was a tremendous fall of snow, and . . . hardly a local resident turned up. This was, perhaps, just as well [because] H.G. Wells arrived with his wife and he invented a game of racing on broomsticks over the polished floor, which I think would have staggered the local gentry.

The guests and their hosts danced on the final night of the party. Outwardly, Stephen appeared as merry as the others, but looking back on the evening, H.G. Wells realized that "he was profoundly weary and ill, if I had been wise enough to see it."

Shortly after the guests had gone to bed, Cora knocked on the door to the room where Wells and his wife were sleeping. Stephen had hemorrhaged from the lungs. There was no telephone at Brede Place, and Cora asked Wells to go for a doctor. "There was a bicycle in the place," Wells later wrote, "and my last clear memory of that fantastic Brede House party is riding out of the cold . . . wintry night into a drizzling dawn along a wet road to call up a doctor."

After the hemorrhage, Stephen worked from his bed until he could be up and around. He was writing an Irish romance about a character named O'Ruddy, grimly grinding out chapter after chapter.

Crane at Brede Place with one of his dogs, August 1899.
(Courtesy of the University of Virginia)

In 1899, war began between Britain and the Dutch Afrikaners, known as "Boers," over control of South Africa. In February of the following year, Stephen wrote a piece for the *New York Journal* protesting the censorship of correspondents in that war. He told the *Journal* that his health had improved, and even asked about a correspondent's assignment. In his heart, however, he knew his days of reporting wars were over. At a luncheon held in his honor that month, one of the guests described him as having that "white, worn-out, restless look [indicating] complete nervous exhaustion."

Nevertheless, by the end of March, Crane had finished twenty-four chapters of the O'Ruddy manuscript. He had experienced no more bleeding, and Cora thought she could leave him long enough to escort Helen Crane home from Paris. (Helen was dropping out of school.) Only two hours after Cora left, Stephen suffered another hemorrhage.

The cook sent a telegram to Paris, and Cora and Helen left immediately for home. Cora wired the American embassy in London for assistance. The secretary at the embassy sent one of England's leading lung specialists to Brede Place. But over the next ten days, Stephen sustained a series of hemorrhages. Cora hired two nurses, and she herself stayed at Stephen's side night and day.

By mid-April, it was clear that Stephen was dying. Cora wrote to Clara Frewen, "He seems to get weaker every day." When the specialist suggested taking Stephen to a sanitarium in Badenweiler, Germany, Cora immediately set about acquiring the money needed to make the trip. She wrote to Pinker, to William Crane, and to any friends she thought might help. Many responded, including Stephen's former agent Paul Revere Reynolds.

In the meantime, Stephen made a new will naming Cora as his sole beneficiary. With that done, only one other thing weighed heavily on his mind. He was concerned about Joseph Conrad, who was also ill and had no money. In the last letter he ever wrote, Stephen asked an old friend if he could pull strings to obtain financial aid from the English government for Conrad. "He is poor and a gentleman and proud." Stephen wrote. "Please do me [this] last favor."

On May 15, Stephen, accompanied by Cora and Helen, two nurses, a local doctor, and his favorite dog, Sponge, left Brede Place for the sanitarium in Germany. They traveled as far as Dover, staying in a hotel there, so that Stephen could rest before making the trip across the English Channel.

At Dover, friends came to see him for the last time. Wells came, noting that "he was thin and gaunt and wasted." Robert Barr, who would reluctantly agree to complete *O'Ruddy* for the dying author, came also. Stephen talked about his approaching death to Barr: "Robert, when you come to the hedge—that we must all go over—it isn't bad. You feel sleepy—and—you don't care. Just a little dreamy curiosity—[as to] which world you're really in—that's all."

Of course, Joseph Conrad came even though he himself was ill. After seeing the wasted shadow Stephen had become, the grieving Conrad told his wife: "It is the end . . . He knows it is all useless. He goes [to the Black Forest] only to please Cora, and he would rather have died at home!"

Nevertheless, Crane did go, arriving at the sanitarium on May 28. He had continued to dictate parts of *O'Ruddy* to Cora, but by June 3 he was beginning to hallucinate. Cora wrote to Moreton Frewen: "My husband's brain is never at rest. He lives over everything and talks aloud constantly. It is too awful to hear him try to change places in the 'open boat!!' "

Two days later, on June 5, 1900, Stephen finally found peace from the restless seeking that had comprised his life. He died in the German sanitarium at three in the morning, leaving behind a legacy of unfulfilled possibilities. He was twenty-eight years old. "His passage on this earth," Joseph Conrad wrote, "was like that of a horseman riding swiftly in the dawn of a day fated to be short and without sunshine."

Stephen Crane died at a tragically young age. Yet he lives on through his books and stories, which are still being read and have deeply influenced many writers who came after him. One of the writers who most felt the impact of Crane's life and work was Ernest Hemingway, also a war correspondent and a novelist who wrote about war. In 1942, Hemingway wrote about Crane's genius:

There was no real literature of the Civil War . . . until

Stephen Crane wrote 'The Red Badge of Courage.' Crane wrote it before he had ever seen any war. But he had read the contemporary accounts, had heard the old soldiers . . . talk, and . . . had seen Matthew Brady's wonderful photographs. Creating his story out of this material he wrote that great boy's dream of war that was . . . truer to how war is than any war the boy who wrote it would ever live to see. It is one of the finest books of our literature.

Major Works

Maggie: A Girl of the Streets. New York: Privately printed, 1893. Revised edition, New York: Appleton, 1896.

The Black Riders. Boston: Copeland and Day, 1895.

The Red Badge of Courage. New York: Appleton, 1895.

George's Mother. New York and London: Edward Arnold, 1896.

The Little Regiment. New York: Appleton, 1896.

The Third Violet. New York: Appleton, 1897.

The Open Boat. New York: Doubleday & McClure, 1898.

War Is Kind. New York: Stokes, 1899.

Active Service. New York: Stokes, 1899.

The Monster. New York and London: Harper, 1899.

Whilomville Stories. New York and London: Harper, 1900.

Wounds in the Rain. New York: Stokes, 1900.

Great Battles of the World. Philadelphia: Lippincott, 1901.

Last Words. London: Digby, Long, 1902.

The O'Ruddy (by Crane and Robert Barr). New York: Stokes, 1903.

The Sullivan County Sketches of Stephen Crane (edited by Melvin Schoberlin). Syracuse, N.Y.: Syracuse Univ. Press, 1949.

The War Dispatches of Stephen Crane (edited by R.W. Stallman and E.R. Hagemann). New York: New York University Press, 1964.

The New York City Sketches of Stephen Crane (edited by Stallman and Hagemann). Ames, Iowa: Iowa State Univ. Press, 1968.

Sullivan County Tales and Sketches (edited by Stallman). Ames, Iowa: Iowa State Univ. Press, 1968.

The Notebook of Stephen Crane (edited by Donald and Ellen Greiner). Charlottesville, Va.: A John Cook Wyllie Memorial Publication, 1969.

Stephen Crane in the West and Mexico (edited by Joseph Katz). Kent, Ohio: Kent State Univ. Press, 1970.

COLLECTIONS:

The Work of Stephen Crane (12 vols. edited by Wilson Follett). New York: Knopf, 1925-1927.

The Collected Poems of Stephen Crane (edited by Follett). New York and London: Knopf, 1930.

The Poems of Stephen Crane (edited by Katz). New York: Cooper Square, 1966.

The Works of Stephen Crane (10 vols. edited by Fredson Bowers). Charlottesville, Va.: Univ. Press of Virginia, 1969-1976.

Timeline

1871—Stephen Crane born in Newark, New Jersey, November 1.

1878—Family moves to Port Jervis, New York. Stephen starts school.

1880—Father dies.

1883—Moves to Asbury Park, New Jersey. Fannie Crane dies.

1884—Agnes Crane dies.

1885-87—Enrolls at Pennington Seminary.

1886—Luther Crane killed in an accident.

1888-90—Attends Claverack College and Hudson River Institute. Begins summer reporting work for Townley Crane's news agency. Essay published in school newspaper.

1890—Enters Lafayette College.

1891—Transfers to Syracuse University. Joins Delta Upsilon fraternity. Plays on the varsity baseball team. Local correspondent for the *Tribune*. Meets Hamlin Garland. Drops out of college. Moves to Edmund's house in Lake View. Explores the slums of lower Manhattan. Mother dies.

1892—Sullivan County tales and sketches published in the *Tribune*. Moves to New York. Revises *Maggie*, a novel begun earlier.

1893—Self-publishes *Maggie: A Girl of the Streets*. Meets William Dean Howells. Begins writing *The Red Badge of Courage*.

1894—Writes Bowery articles. Completes *George's Mother*. Shows Hamlin Garland his poems and the manuscript of *The Red Badge of Courage*. Negotiates with Boston publisher Copeland and Day over *The Black Riders*. Sells *The Red Badge of Courage* to the Bacheller newspaper syndicate.

1895—Travels to the West and Mexico as a feature writer for the Bacheller syndicate. Meets Willa Cather. *Black Riders* is published. Becomes a member of the Lantern Club. Writes *The Third Violet*. *The Red Badge of Courage* is published in book form.

1896—*George's Mother*, *The Little Regiment*, and a sanitized version of *Maggie* are published. Testifies for prostitute Dora Clark. Hired by Bacheller to report on the uprising in Cuba. Meets Cora Taylor at the Hotel de Dream. Arranges passage for Cuba aboard the *Commodore*.

1897—*Commodore* sinks enroute to Cuba. Spends thirty hours drifting on the open sea. Writes "The Open Boat." Hired by the *New York Journal* to cover the Greco-Turkish War. *The Third Violet* published. Settles in England with Cora. Meets Joseph Conrad. Writes "The Monster," "Death and the Child," and "The Bride Comes to Yellow Sky."

1898—Completes "The Blue Hotel." Returns to New York. Covers the Spanish-American War for the *New York World*. Publishes *The Open Boat and Other Tales*. Reports on the Battle of San Juan Hill. Leaves the *New York World*. Contracts with the *New York Journal* to cover the Puerto Rican campaign. Disappears into Havana for three months. Sails for England on December 31.

1899—Rents Brede Place. Publishes *War Is Kind*. Completes *Active Service*. Writes the Whilomville stories. Finishes Cuban War stories and sketches for *Wounds in the Rain*. Personal debts become increasingly unmanageable. Suffers a tubercular hemorrhage.

1900—Continues financial struggles. Publishes *Whilomville Stories* and *Wounds in the Rain*. Experiences further hemorrhaging from the lungs. Taken by Cora to a tuberculosis sanitarium in Germany's Black Forest at Badenweiler. Works intermittently on *O'Ruddy*. Dies June 5 in the sanitarium. Body is returned to the United States for burial at Evergreen Cemetery in Hillside, New Jersey.

Notes

CHAPTER ONE: PREACHER'S KID

p. 10, Crane's eight surviving brothers and sister were in order of birth: Mary Helen, George Peck, Jonathan Townley, William Howe, Agnes Elizabeth, Edmund Bryan, Wilbur Fiske, and Luther.

p. 10, Stephen's father, Jonathon Townley Crane, graduated from the College of New Jersey (later Princeton University) in 1843, and in 1856 he received a doctor of divinity degree from New Jersey's Dickinson College.

p. 14, James Fenimore Cooper was an early nineteenth century writer. His popular novels featured frontier hero Natty Bumppo in an adventure series set on the New York frontier in the 1740s.

CHAPTER TWO: LEAVING HOME

p. 19, Helen Crane was annually reelected president of the Asbury Park and Ocean Grove WCTU until she resigned in 1891.

p. 20, Bright's disease is a disease of the kidneys.

p. 20, Agnes died at her brother Edmund's house in Rutherford, New Jersey—sixty miles away from Asbury Park. The family may have arranged for this move in order to shield Stephen.

p. 21, "Uncle Jake and the Bell Handle" was published after Crane's death.

p. 22, The unsigned sketch appeared simultaneously in the *Daily Spray* and the *Philadelphia Press.*

p. 24, Stephen never learned certain grammatical principles, and he never learned to spell. He particularly had trouble with "ie" words, never sure whether the "i" or the "e" came first.

p. 27, Sir Henry Morton Stanley was an American journalist and explorer who traced the source of the Nile River and found the lost explorer David Livingstone.

p. 27, Stephen had transferred his Delta Upsilon membership from Lafayette College to Syracuse.

p. 28, Crane received an A in English Literature—the one class he enrolled in at Syracuse.

CHAPTER THREE: LESSONS OF ASBURY PARK

p. 32, Louis C. Senger Jr. was an artist friend of Crane's from Port Jervis.

p. 33, William Fletcher Johnson had published some of the pieces Stephen wrote when he was a student at Syracuse.

p. 34, Garland's first book was titled *Main-Traveled Roads.*

p. 34, Howell's books dealt with previously taboo subjects such as divorce and corruption in the business world.

p. 36, Lily Brandon Monroe's husband later destroyed these manuscripts in a jealous rage.

p. 38, Whitelaw Reid had succeeded Horace Greeley as the *Tribune's* publisher. He was the running mate of incumbent president Benjamin Harrison. They lost the election to Grover Cleveland.

p. 38, Garland was seven years older than Crane.

CHAPTER FOUR: MAGGIE'S TOWN

p. 40, Thoreau's sojourn at Walden Pond produced one of America's literary masterpieces: *Walden; or, Life in the Woods.*

p. 40, *The Guilded Age* was the title of a novel by Mark Twain and Charles Dudley Warner published in 1873. It satirized the shallow materialism of industrial America in the late nineteenth century and the corruption in American politics.

p. 40, In 1890, Jacob Riis, a crusading reformer who knew the
  overcrowded, disease-ridden tenements of New York first-
  hand, authored a book describing slum conditions.
  The book, called *How the Other Half Lives,* was illustrated
  with Riis's own photographs.

p. 41, The Pendennis nickname stemmed from a novel by
  British author William Makepeace Thackeray titled *The
  History of Pendennis.* The novel traced the youthful,
  worldly pursuits of its hero, Arthur Pendennis, including
  his first love affair and his employment as a London
  journalist.

p. 42, The profanity in *Maggie: A Girl of the Streets* consisted
  of "hells" and "damns," plus approximately seven uses of
  the name for the deity dialectically spelled "Gawd."

p. 43, Corwin Knapp Linson was an American painter and
  illustrator who had studied in Paris. At the time Crane met
  him, he had already achieved limited success. He would
  illustrate several of Crane's early stories.

p. 46, *Century's* Civil War series had run from November
  1884 through November 1887. The magazines provided
  much of the military background for *The Red Badge of
  Courage*.

p. 46, Hamlin Garland had encouraged Crane to send a copy
  of *Maggie* to Howells.

p. 46, Emily Dickinson had only seven poems published
  during her lifetime, but nearly 1,800 poems were
  discovered after her death in 1886. The first volume of her
  work was published in 1890, the second in 1891.

CHAPTER FIVE: THE RED AND THE BLACK

p. 49, *George's Mother* was set in the same slum atmosphere
  as *Maggie: A Girl of the Streets*.

p. 49, The article on shelter for the homeless was titled "An
  Experiment in Misery."

p. 52, The "red badge" in *The Red Badge of Courage* refers to
  a wound received in combat.

p. 54, William was now a successful lawyer.

p. 54, Edmund's home was near the Hartwood Village Club, a 3,600-acre tract of land over which Edmund served as custodian. The house itself belonged to William, who had acquired it as payment for legal services to the club.

p. 56, Frederic Gordon provided the artwork for the cover of *Black Riders and Other Lines*.

p. 56, Crane dedicated *Black Riders* to Hamlin Garland.

CHAPTER SIX: NEW HORIZONS

p. 60, Willa Cather, still a student, worked part-time for the *Journal*. She went on to become a Pulitzer-prize winning author noted for novels that portrayed frontier life on the American plains.

p. 63, "One Dash" is a phrase used to describe an all or nothing roll of the dice.

p. 63, "The Bride Comes to Yellow Sky" was written in 1897 and "The Blue Hotel" in 1898.

p. 64, Nelson Green, an artist, later became a cartoonist for *Puck* magazine.

p. 64, Dentists at that time were not formally trained, and drilling and extractions were performed without anesthesia—which may explain Crane's reluctance to see a dentist.

p. 65, Hubbard did not keep his word. He never ran the ad for *The Red Badge of Courage*.

p. 65, Appleton's contract for *The Red Badge of Courage* offered Crane no advance money and only a ten percent royalty with no stipulation for an increase if the book went to larger sales. Nor was there any provision for sharing proceeds of foreign sales.

p. 67, Crane received no money for the British edition of *The Red Badge of Courage*. However, two years later when the English publisher learned this, he sent Crane an honorarium of thirty pounds.

CHAPTER SEVEN: "I AM MOSTLY, AFRAID"

p. 69, The Civil War ended five and one-half years before Crane was born.

p. 69, The "abuse" referred primarily to critic's reviews of *Black Riders*.

p. 73, The "other stories" in *The Little Regiment and Other Stories* included: "The Veteran," "Three Miraculous Soldiers," "An Indiana Campaign," and "An Episode of War."

p. 74, Crane bought Peanuts from Elbert Hubbard, publisher of the *Philistine*.

p. 74, The British publisher of *Maggie* changed its subtitle "*A Story of New York*," to *"A Girl of the Streets."*

p. 74, The infamous Tenderloin district (located between Fourth and Seventh Avenues and extending from Fourteenth Street to Forty-second Street) supposedly acquired its name from remarks a policeman made after being transferred there. Indicating the acceptance of bribes and payoffs, the officer reportedly said that now instead of eating only chuck steak, he would be able to afford the more choice tenderloin cut.

p. 77, Thirteen years after Crane died, Officer Charles Becker was executed for hiring the murder of a gambler who had threatened to expose Becker's connections with the underworld.

p. 77, Later writers, such as Ernest Hemingway, would follow Crane's example and work as war correspondents in order to acquire the necessary background for novel writing.

CHAPTER EIGHT: ADRIFT

p. 78, Many Americans supported the Cuban rebels, but America itself was not officially at war. Therefore, ships carrying contraband needed to avoid the U.S. Navy as well as Spanish gunboats.

p. 78, Crane appointed William executor of his estate and divided his assets among his brothers.

p. 79, The Hotel de Dream was named after its former owner, Ethel Dreme. Cora's biographer has pointed out that technically the establishment was not a house of prostitution because the women who worked there did not live on the premises.

p. 84, Paul Reynolds's impressive array of clients also included George Bernard Shaw, Joseph Conrad, and Leo Tolstoy.

p. 85, The Greco-Turkish War centered around control of the island of Crete, then under Turkish rule. Crete had rebelled against the Turks and requested union with Greece.

p. 85, Cora apparently left town without paying her bills, because soon after her departure, a warrant was issued against her for non-payment of debts.

CHAPTER NINE: EXILE

p. 89, Crane later wrote a series of stories set in the fictional town of Wilhomville, all written about children but not for children.

p. 90, Joseph Conrad, whose real name was Jozef Teador Konrad Korzeniowski, was born in Poland but had become a British subject a year before he and Crane met.

p. 92, There is no record of the amount of the settlement with Amy Leslie.

p. 94, The signalmen, also called wigwaggers, flashed their lanterns to send messages to ships. Unfortunately, the lanterns gave the enemy a clear target.

p. 94, The colleague was *World* reporter Ernest McCready.

p. 94, The official name of the Rough Riders was the First U.S. Volunteer Cavalry Regiment.

p. 96, Reporters had not expected anything to happen at San Juan Hill, so they could only watch from the foothills below. Stephen developed what little he did see into his longest report of the war, "Stephen Crane's Vivid Story of the Battle of San Juan."

p. 97, The *World* refused to pay for Crane's new suit.

p. 97, A peace treaty between Spain and the United States was signed August 12, 1898.

p. 97, Either Dr. Trudeau made a mistake in his evaluation, or Stephen had asked him not to alarm Cora.

p. 97, What happened to the $3,000 Crane had earlier

received from the *World* is uncertain.

p. 98, Cora had learned of Crane's so-called disappearance from a Florida newspaper article sent to her in September.

CHAPTER TEN: THE FUTURE UNLIVED

p. 104, Ford Maddox Ford was at that time still using his birth name Hueffer.

p. 104, Technically, Cora could be considered English because of her marriage to Stewart. But it was a misleading statement, made because Crane did not want his family to know about Cora's questionable past.

p. 104, Some biographers speculate that Crane worked so hard because he hoped to provide for Cora's future.

p. 108, The British undersecretary of war was George Wyndham, who had once written an article praising *The Red Badge of Courage*.

p. 109, Crane never completed his novel on the American Revolution.

p. 113, William Crane told Cora that he could not afford to help.

p. 113, Crane's will stipulated that if Cora died or remarried, half of Stephen's income would be held in trust for his namesake, Edmund's infant son Stephen, and the other half equally divided between Edmund and William.

p. 113, The old friend Crane wrote to about Conrad was Sanford Bennett. He had influential political friends. Stephen had met Bennett in Paris in 1897, when he was on his way to cover the war in Greece.

p. 114, In a moment of lucidity, Stephen told Cora he wanted to be buried in his parents' burial plot in New Jersey.

p. 114, When Crane died, he was the same age his sister Agnes had been when she died.

p. 114, On June 17, 1900, Cora boarded a ship to accompany Stephen's body home for burial. As requested, he was buried alongside his parents.

Sources

CHAPTER ONE: PREACHER'S KID

p. 9, "I expect to make a sincere . . ." R.W. Stallman and Lillian Gilkes, eds., *Stephen Crane: Letters* (New York: New York Univ. Press, 1960), 105.

p. 10, "This morning . . . our fourteenth child was born." Thomas A. Gullason, ed., *Stephen Crane's Career: Perspectives and Evaluations* (New York: New York Univ. Press, 1972), 20.

p. 10, "morbid love of excitement" Stallman and Gilkes, *Letters*, 5.

p. 12, "He liked all kinds of animals . . ." Ibid., 243.

p. 12, "I . . . think a good saddle-horse . . . " Ibid., 117.

p. 12, "everybody as soon as he could walk . . ." R.W. Stallman, *Stephen Crane: A Biography* (New York: George Braziller, Inc., 1968), 4.

p. 12, "[She] was a very religious woman . . ." Stallman and Gilkes, *Letters*, 241-242.

p. 12, "One of my sisters . . ." Ibid., 242.

p. 14, "she ought to stay at home . . ." Stanley Wertheim and Paul Sorrentino, eds, *The Crane Log: A Documentary Life of Stephen Crane, 1871-1900* (New York: G.K. Hall, 1994), 22.

p. 14, "started to [swim] . . ." Wertheim and Sorrentino, *Log*, 10.
p. 14, "Stevie was making weird marks . . ." Ibid., 8.
p. 16, "Last Christmas they gave me . . ." James B. Colvert, *Stephen Crane* (New York: Harcourt Brace Jovanovich, 1984), 9.
p. 17, "They tell me . . ." Stallman and Gilkes, *Letters*, 243.

CHAPTER TWO: LEAVING HOME
p. 18, "he worked himself to death . . ." Stallman and Gilkes, *Letters*, 243.
p. 18, "He used to take me driving . . ." Ibid., 243.
p. 19, "The Summer Mecca of Methodist Americans," Stallman, *A Biography,* 11.
p. 21, "Ma says . . ." Ibid., 10.
p. 22, "As the professor called me a liar . . ." Linda H. Davis, *Badge of Courage: The Life of Stephen Crane* (New York: Houghton Mifflin Company, 1998), 22.
p. 22, "Nothing would induce him . . ." Ibid., 22.
p. 24, "Students roamed . . ." Colvert, *Stephen Crane*, 11.
p. 24, "the happiest period of my life," Ibid., 12
p. 24, "I never learned anything . . ." Ibid.
p. 24, "a law unto himself" Davis, *Badge of Courage*, 26.
p. 26, "his name was never among . . ." Ibid., 27.
p. 26, "Of course, you were joking . . ." Stallman and Gilkes, *Letters*, 119.
p. 26, "the stripes of a corporal on his natty uniform." Davis, *Badge of Courage*, 25.
p. 28, "Mark my words . . ." Stallman and Gilkes, *Letters*, 7.
p. 28, "So long, old man . . ." Ibid., 7.
p. 28, "I found mining and engineering . . ." Colvert, *Stephen Crane*, 16.
p. 28, "We all counted on him . . ." Ibid., 16.
p. 28 "in a cab and cloud of tobacco smoke." Stallman, *A Biography*, 27
p. 28, "Crane . . . has entered the University . . ." Colvert, *Stephen Crane*, 19.

p. 29, "more to play baseball than to study." Davis, *Badge of Courage*, 32.

p. 29, "small-chested and droop-shouldered . . ." Ibid.

p. 30, "What does St. Paul say, Mr. Crane . . ." Ibid., 34.

p. 30, "turn grindstone for [sharpening] the kitchen knives . . ." Ibid.

p. 30, "When I ought to have been at [class] . . ." Ibid., 33.

p. 30, "His future was in literature." Ibid., 34.

p. 31, "I did little work at school . . ." Stallman and Gilkes, *Letters*, 108-109.

CHAPTER THREE: LESSONS OF ASBURY PARK

p. 32, "wonderful yarn spinners." Davis, *Badge of Courage*, 38.

p. 32, "little grotesque tales of the woods." Christopher Benfey, *The Double Life of Stephen Crane* (New York: Alfred A. Knopf, 1992), 56.

p. 33, "The beach, the avenues . . ." Wertheim and Sorrentino, *Log*, 63.

p. 34, "the truthful treatment of commonplace material." John A. Garrity, ed., *Encyclopedia of American Biography* (New York: Harper and Row, 1974), 546.

p. 34, "all alone a little creed . . ." Stallman and Gilkes, *Letters*, 31.

p. 34, "creed was identical . . ." Ibid.

p. 34, "[Howells] stands for all that is . . ." Fredson Bowers, ed., *University of Virginia Edition of the Works of Stephen Crane*, Vol. 8 (Charlottesville: Univ. Press of Virginia, 1969-1976), 507-508.

p. 34, "Crane loved this [outdoor] life . . ." Wertheim and Sorrentino, *Log*, 65.

p. 35, "the bums and outcasts . . ." Van Wyck Brooks, *The Confident Years: 1885-1915* (New York: E.P. Dutton and Company, Inc., 1955), 130.

p. 36, "bewitchingly lovely" Stallman, *A Biography*, 47.

p. 36, "whenever she saw the ocean . . ." Stallman and Gilkes, *Letters*, 20.

p. 37, "summer gowns, lace parasols . . ." Bowers, *Virginia Edition*, Vol. 8, 522.

p. 37, "The bona fide Asbury Parker . . ." Ibid.

p. 37, "[It] creates nothing. It does not make . . ." Ibid., 521.

p. 38, "un-American" Wertheim and Sorrentino, *Log*, 78.

p. 38, "[seize] upon any opportunity. . ." Ibid., 79.

p. 38, "This young man has a hankering for . . ." Ibid., 80.

p. 38, "No! You've got to feel the things . . ." Davis, *Badge of Courage*, 51.

p. 39, "I want you to read . . ." Wertheim and Sorrentino, *Log*, 80.

CHAPTER FOUR: MAGGIE'S TOWN

p. 40, "I wish to meet . . ." Robert D. Richardson Jr., *Henry Thoreau: A Life of the Mind* (Los Angeles: Univ. of California Press, 1986), 153.

p. 40, "I decided that the nearer a writer gets . . ." Stallman and Gilkes, *Letters*, 78.

p. 41, "As the story, a sordid tale . . ." Wertheim and Sorrentino, *Log*, 81.

p. 42, "Breakfast 13 cents . . ." Bowers, *Virginia Edition*, Vol. 8, 279.

p. 42, "You mean that the story's too honest." Stallman and Gilkes, *Letters*, 16.

p. 43, "A Girl of the Streets . . ." Wertheim and Sorrentino, *Log*, 83.

p. 44, "Steve reveled in the use of words . . ." Corwin K. Linson, *My Stephen Crane*, Edwin H. Cady, ed. (Syracuse, N.Y.: Syracuse Univ. Press, 1958), 31.

p. 44, "In memory . . . I see . . ." Ibid., 34.

p. 44, "wished to disguise . . ." Wertheim and Sorrentino, *Log*, 84.

p. 44, "commonest name I could think of . . ." Linson, *My Stephen Crane*, 21.

p. 44, "I remember how I looked forward . . ." Stallman and Gilkes, *Letters*, 79.

p. 45, "It is inevitable that you will . . ." Ibid., 14.

p. 45, "Mustard-yellow piles" Wertheim and Sorrentino, *Log*, 86.

p. 45, "The animals apologize . . ." Linson, *My Stephen Crane*, 27.

p. 45, "Cheese it . . ." Wertheim and Sorrentino, *Log*, 86, 88.

p. 46, "squatting like an Indian . . ." Linson, *My Stephen Crane*, 37.

p. 46, "I wonder . . . that *some* of these fellows . . ." Ibid., 37.

p. 46, "Having recieved [sic] no reply . . ." Stallman and Gilkes, *Letters*, 16

p. 46, "From the glance . . ." Ibid., 17.

p. 47, "Well, at least I've done something." Wertheim and Sorrentino, *Log*, 90.

p. 47, "So I think I can say . . ." Ibid.

CHAPTER FIVE: THE RED AND THE BLACK

p. 48, "As soon as the story began . . ." Ibid., 92.

p. 48, "The upper floors were filled . . ." Ibid., 93.

p. 49, "It is beyond me to free myself . . ." Stallman and Gilkes, *Letters*, 22.

p. 49, "looking haggard and almost ill," Linson, *My Stephen Crane*, 58.

p. 50, "How would I know . . ." Ibid.

p. 50, "We went as hoboes . . ." Wertheim and Sorrentino, *Log*, 97.

p. 50, "delight and amazement" Ibid., 98.

p. 50, "I've got five or six all in a little row . . ." Stallman, *A Biography*, 90.

p. 51, "too orphic [mystic]" Wertheim and Sorrentino, *Log*, 113.

p. 51, "I wish you had given them . . ." Stallman and Gilkes, *Letters*, 31.

p. 51, "fired them off to Copeland and Day," Joseph Katz, ed., *The Poems of Stephen Crane* (New York: Cooper Square Publishers, Inc.,1966), Introduction, xxv.

p. 51, "I daren't tell you how much I value . . ." Wertheim and Sorrentino, *Log*, 101.

p. 51, "in hock" Davis, *Badge of Courage*, 85.

p. 52, "overly critical of business interests." Wertheim and Sorrentino, *Log*, 108.

p. 54, "The birds didn't want the truth . . ." Linson, *My Stephen Crane*, 70.

p. 54, "Stephen was [as] happy there . . ." Ibid., 75.

p. 55, "I would like to hear from you . . ." Wertheim and Sorrentino, *Log*, 111.

p. 55, "Stephen was a furious loafer . . ." Linson, *My Stephen Crane*, 80.

p. 55, "We children would have remembered . . ." Ibid., 77-78.

p. 55, "It seems to me that you cut . . ." Katz, *Poems*, Introduction, xxvii.

p. 56, "Mr. Stephen Crane's little story . . ." Wertheim and Sorrentino, *Log*, 113.

p. 57, "Mr. Howells and Hamlin Garland . . ." Irving Bacheller, *Coming Up the Road: Memories of a North Country Boyhood* (Indianapolis: Bobbs-Merrill, 1928), 277.

p. 57, "My wife and I spent . . ." Ibid., 278.

p. 57, "I can [now] write . . ." Wertheim and Sorrentino, *Log*, 116.

p. 57, "Somebody has written clean from California . . ." Stephen Crane, "The Red Badge of Courage" (A Facsimile Reproduction of the New York *Press* Appearance of December 9, 1894 with an Introduction and Textual Notes by Joseph Katz. Gainesville, Fla.: Scholars' Facsimiles & Reprints, 1967), 27.

p. 58, "one rather long story . . ." Wertheim and Sorrentino, *Log*, 118.

p. 58, "I have just crawled . . ." Ibid., 116.

p. 58, "Stephen Crane is a new name now . . ." Ibid., 117.

CHAPTER SIX: NEW HORIZONS

p. 60, "This was the first man of letters . . ." Willa Cather, "When I Knew Stephen Crane," in *Stephen Crane: A Collection of Critical Essays*, Maurice Bassan, ed. (Englewood Cliffs, New Jersey: Prentice-Hall, Inc., 1967), 12.

p. 60, "He was thin . . ." Cather, "When I Knew," 12-14.

p. 61, "The thermometer . . . registers . . ." Joseph Katz, ed., *Stephen Crane in the West and Mexico*, (Kent, Ohio: Kent State Univ. Press, 1970), 9.

p. 61, "[He] was moody most of the time . . ." Cather, "When I Knew," 14.

p. 61, "led a double literary life . . ." Ibid., 15.

p. 61, "The detail of a thing has to filter . . ." Ibid., 16.

p. 61, "steadfast and unyielding . . ." Katz, *Stephen Crane in the West*, 14.

p. 62, "Over the river . . ." Colvert, *Stephen Crane*, 82

p. 62, "I would tell you of many . . ." Stallman and Gilkes, *Letters*, 54.

p. 62, "Indian girls with bare brown . . ." Katz, *Stephen Crane in the West*, 72.

p. 62, "crimson, purple, orange . . ." Ibid., 72.

p. 62, "The most worthless literature of the world . . ." Davis, *Badge of Courage*, 112.

p. 63, "the color of a brick side-walk." Ibid., 114.

p. 63, "The most remarkable thing . . ." Wertheim and Sorrentino, *Log*, 132.

p. 64, "got by largely on a diet . . ." Davis, *Badge of Courage*, 120.

p. 64, "We fellows thought . . ." Ibid., 120-21.

p. 64, "a bold—sometimes too bold . . ." *Concise Dictionary of American Literary Biography, Realism, Naturalism, and Local Color*, Vol. 2, (Detroit: Gale Research, Inc., 1988), 101.

p. 64, "so much trash." Wertheim and Sorrentino, *Log*, 135.

p. 64, "At our dinners . . ." Bacheller, *Coming up the Road*, 281.

p. 65, "I saw a man making a fool . . ." D.H. Dickason, "Stephen Crane and the *Philistine*," *American Literature: A Journal of Literary History, Criticism, and Bibliography*, Vol. 15, (November 1943): 281.

p. 65, "we will take it all back . . ." Stanley Wertheim and Paul Sorrentino, eds., *The Correspondence of Stephen Crane*, Vol. 1, (New York: Columbia Univ. Press, 1988), 109.

p. 66, "I am cruising around the woods . . ." Davis, *Badge of Courage*, 126.

p. 66, "There are six girls . . ." Wertheim and Sorrentino, *Log*, 146.

p. 66, "a picture which seems . . ." Ibid.,143-44.

p. 66, "splendid and all aglow . . ." Ibid.,146.

p. 66, "the most realistic and ghastly . . ." Ibid.

p. 66, "Recognizing . . . your genius . . ." Wertheim and Sorrentino, *Correspondence*, Vol. 1, 137.

p. 67, "Write me at once . . ." Ibid., 149.

p. 67, "pride and arrogance . . ." Stallman and Gilkes, *Letters*, 73.

p. 67, "You ought to see the effect . . ." Ibid.

p. 67, "You represent a 'cause' and . . ." Wertheim and Sorrentino, *Log*, 150.

p. 68, "We think so highly of your work . . ." Bowers, *Virginia Edition*, Vol. 2, Introduction, xci.

p. 68, "It's pretty rotten work . . ." Davis, *Badge of Courage*, 138.

CHAPTER SEVEN: "I AM MOSTLY, AFRAID"

p. 69, I am slightly rattled . . ." Wertheim and Sorrentino, *Correspondence*, Vol. I, 192.

p. 70, "I had grown used to . . ." Ibid., 191.

p. 70, "You have been . . ." Stallman and Gilkes, *Letters*, 101.

p. 70, "At my publishers yesterday . . ." Ibid., 105.

p. 72, "I think it is as well . . ." Ibid., 106.

p. 72, "I am engaged in . . ." Ibid., 111.

p. 72, "It is awfully hard," Wertheim and Sorrentino, *Correspondence*, Vol. I, 175.

p. 72, "I feel for you when I think . . ." Stallman and Gilkes, *Letters*, 108.

p. 73, "It is not that people . . ." Ibid., 120.

p. 73, "If there is a joy of living . . ." Ibid.

p. 73, "deeply in love with her." Davis, *Badge of Courage*, 149.

p. 74, "I have dispensed . . ." Stallman and Gilkes, *Letters*, 112.

p. 75, "perfectly respectable" Davis, *Badge of Courage*, 156.

p. 75, "If you monkey with . . ." Ibid., 157.

p. 75, "an old offender." Ibid.

p. 75, "Your Honor, I know . . ." Ibid.

p. 76, "I am Stephen Crane . . ." Ibid., 157.

p. 76, "He wore No Red Badge . . ." Ibid., 158.

p. 76, "Brave as His Hero," Ibid.
p. 76, "Stephen Crane is respectfully . . ." Ibid., 158-59.
p. 76, "The chances are . . ." Ibid., 159.
p. 77, "the longest trial ever held . . ." Ibid., 166.

CHAPTER EIGHT: ADRIFT
p. 78, "acted like a man of honor . . ." Wertheim and Sorrentino, *Correspondence*, Vol. I, 266.
p. 79, "In case you see Amy . . ." Ibid., 267.
p. 79, "I think of you, night and day . . ." Wertheim and Sorrentino, *Log*, 229.
p. 79, "Fact is, she was a cut above . . ." Davis, *Badge of Courage*, 177.
p. 80, "I guess I won't need them . . ." Ibid., 180.
p. 82, "They rolled in on us . . ." Ibid., 181.
p. 83, "We were afraid to trust ourselves . . ." Stallman, *A Biography*, 251.
p. 83, "A night on the sea in an open boat . . ." Davis, *Badge of Courage*, 184.
p. 83, "He dashed into the water . . ." Wertheim and Sorrentino, *Log*, 236.
p. 84, "Thank God [you're] safe . . ." Stallman, *A Biography*, 254.
p. 84, "That man Crane is the spunkiest . . ." Wertheim and Sorrentino, *Log*, 238.
p. 85, "I have changed all . . ." Wertheim and Sorrentino, *Correspondence*, Vol. I, 281.
p. 86, "The roll of musketry fire . . ." Edwin H. Cady, *Stephen Crane* (Boston: Twayne Publishers, A Division of G.K. Hall & Co., 1980), 63.
p. 86, "all right" Wertheim and Sorrentino, *Correspondence*, Vol. I, 283.
p. 86, "Reserves coming up passed . . ." Colvert, *Stephen Crane*, 114.
p. 88, "fat waddling puppy" Wertheim and Sorrentino, *Log*, 254.
p. 88, "Velestino, the Journal Dog" Ibid.

CHAPTER NINE: EXILE

p. 90, "far from being a great writer . . ." Wertheim and
    Sorrentino, *Log*, 258.

p. 90, "the front rank of English . . ." Ibid., 261.

p. 90, "The book is simply great . . ." Wertheim and Sorrentino,
    Correspondence, Vol. I, 310.

p. 90, "We have no sense . . ." Colvert, *Stephen Crane*, 120.

p. 91, "I will allow you ten percent . . ." Stallman and Gilkes,
    Letters, 144.

p. 92, "I am just thinking how easy . . ." Ibid., 148.

p. 92, "For heaven's sake raise . . ." Wertheim and Sorrentino,
    Log, 282.

p. 92, "Amy Leslie has brought a suit . . ." Ibid., 285.

p. 92, "To my mind . . . it is a daisy. . ." Stallman and
    Gilkes, *Letters*, 171-72.

p. 93, "age 26 . . . occupation journalist . . ." Wertheim and
    Sorrentino, *Log*, 297.

p. 94, "When one of these men . . ." R.W. Stallman and E.R.
    Hagemann, eds., *The War Dispatches of Stephen Crane*
    (New York: New York Univ. Press, 1964), 149.

p. 94, "When I regained consciousness . . ." Wertheim and
    Sorrentino, *Log*, 318.

p. 96, "[He was] identified . . . in my thoughts . . ." Stallman
    and Hagemann, *War Dispatches*, 285.

p. 97, "Your husband had a slight evidence . . ." Davis,
    Badge of Courage, 272.

p. 97, "shambling . . . hollow-cheeked . . ." Wertheim and
    Sorrentino, *Log*, 333.

p. 98, "I was at a hotel . . ." Wertheim and Sorrentino,
    Correspondence, Vol. II, 355-56.

p. 98, "I cannot help vanishing . . ." Benfey, *Double Life*, 11.

p. 100, "If I dont [sic] receive . . ." Davis, *Badge of Courage*, 286.

p. 101, "He strikes me now . . ." Wertheim and Sorrentino,
    Log, 359.

CHAPTER TEN: THE FUTURE UNLIVED

p. 103, "borrow money from . . ." Wertheim and Sorrentino, *Correspondence*, Vol. II, 419.

p. 103, "I hope that the perfect quiet . . ." Stallman and Gilkes, *Letters*, 203.

p. 103, "lice" Wertheim and Sorrentino, *Correspondence*, Vol. II, 407.

p. 103, "He was beset by people . . ." Wertheim and Sorrentino, *Log*, 386.

p. 104, "Yes, it is true . . ." Wertheim and Sorrentino, *Correspondence*, Vol. II, 416.

p. 105, "feverishly anxious . . ." Wertheim and Sorrentino, *Log*, 385.

p. 105, "If you think I am not hustling . . ." Wertheim and Sorrentino, *Correspondence*, Vol. II, 446.

p. 106, "But sometimes I think I cant . . ." Ibid.

p. 106, "being sent forth into the world . . ." Wertheim and Sorrentino, *Log*, 382.

p. 106, "Either Mr. Crane is insulting . . ." Ibid., 385.

p. 108, "Please have the kindness . . ." Wertheim and Sorrentino, *Correspondence*, Vol. II, 504.

p. 108, "At present I feel like . . ." Ibid., 515.

p. 109, "sure and quick money." Stallman, *A Biography*, 459.

p. 109, "I confess that you are becoming . . ." Wertheim and Sorrentino, *Log*, 404.

p. 109, "a double extra special good thing." Ibid., 405.

p. 109, "one man's reaction . . ." Chester L. Wolford, *Stephen Crane, A Study of the Short Fiction* (Boston: Twayne Publishers, A Division of G.K. Hall & Co., 1989), 79.

p. 110, "[Crane] had invited . . ." Stallman and Gilkes, *Letters*, 343.

p. 110, "he was profoundly weary and ill . . ." Colvert, *Stephen Crane*, 158.

p. 110, "There was a bicycle . . ." Wertheim and Sorrentino, *Log*, 414.

p. 112, "white, worn-out, restless look . . ." Davis, *Badge of Courage*, 319.

p. 112, "He seems to get weaker . . ." Ibid., 322.

p. 113, "He is poor and a gentleman . . ." Stallman and Gilkes, *Letters*, 283-284.

p. 113, "he was thin and gaunt . . ." Davis, *Badge of Courage*, 326.

p. 113, "Robert, when you come to the hedge . . ." Ibid., 327.

p. 114, "It is the end . . ." Ibid., 327.

p. 114, "My husband's brain . . ." Ibid., 329.

p. 114, "His passage on this earth . . ." Gullason, *Career*, 136.

p. 114, "There was no real literature . . ." Ernest Hemingway, ed., *Men at War, The Best War Stories of all Time* (New York: Crown Publishers, 1942), Introduction, xv.

Bibliography

Bacheller, Irving. *Coming up the Road: Memories of a North Country Boyhood.* Indianapolis: Bobbs-Merrill, 1928.

Beer, Thomas. *Stephen Crane: A Study in American Letters.* New York: Knopf, 1923.

Benfey, Christopher. *The Double Life of Stephen Crane.* New York: Knopf, 1988.

Berryman, John. *Stephen Crane.* New York: Sloane, 1950.

Brooks, Van Wyck. *The Confident Years: 1885-1915.* New York: E.P. Dutton and Company, Inc., 1955.

Cady, Edwin H. *Stephen Crane.* New York: Twayne Publishers, Inc., 1980.

Cather, Willa. "When I Knew Stephen Crane," in *Stephen Crane: A Collection of Critical Essays.* Edited by Maurice Bassan. Englewood Cliffs, N.J.: Prentice-Hall, Inc., 1967.

Cazemajou, Jean. *Stephen Crane (1871-1900).* Minneapolis: Univ. of Minnesota Press, 1969.

Colvert, James B. *Stephen Crane.* New York: Harcourt Brace Jovanovich, 1984.

Conrad, Jessie. *Joseph Conrad and his Circle.* Port Washington, N.Y.: Kennikat Press, 1964.

The Correspondence of Stephen Crane, Vols. I, II. Edited by Stanley Wertheim and Paul Sorrentino. New York: Columbia Univ. Press, 1988.

The Crane Log: A Documentary Life of Stephen Crane, 1871-1900. Edited by Stanley Wertheim and Paul Sorrentino. New York: G.K. Hall, 1994.

Crane, Stephen. *University of Virginia Edition of the Works of Stephen Crane*. Edited by Fredson Bowers. 10 vols. Charlottesville: Univ. Press of Virginia, 1969-1976.

─────. *The Poems of Stephen Crane*. Edited by Joseph Katz. New York: Cooper Square Publishers, Inc., 1966.

Davis, Linda H. *Badge of Courage: The Life of Stephen Crane*. New York: Houghton Mifflin Company, 1998.

Dickason, D.H. "Stephen Crane and the *Philistine*" *American Literature: A Journal of Literary History, Criticism, and Bibliography*, Vol. 15, November 1943.

Encyclopedia of American Biography. Edited by John A. Garraty. New York: Harper and Row, 1974.

Gilkes, Lillian. *Cora Crane: A Biography of Mrs. Stephen Crane*. Bloomington: Indiana Univ. Press, 1960.

Holton, Milne. *Cylinder of Vision: The Fiction and Journalistic Writings of Stephen Crane*. Baton Rouge: Louisiana State Univ. Press, 1972.

Linson, Corwin K. *My Stephen Crane*. Edited by Edwin H. Cady. Syracuse, N.Y.: Syracuse Univ. Press, 1958.

Men at War, The Best War Stories of All Time. Edited by Ernest Hemingway. New York: Crown Publishers, 1942.

Monteiro, George. *Stephen Crane's Blue Badge of Courage*. Baton Rouge: Louisiana State Univ. Press, 2000.

Readings on Stephen Crane. Edited by Bonnie Szumski. San Diego: Greenhaven Press, Inc., 1998.

Richardson, Robert D. Jr. *Henry Thoreau: A Life of the Mind*. Los Angeles: Univ. of California Press, 1986.

Stallman, R.W. *Stephen Crane: A Biography*. New York: George Braziller, Inc., 1968.

Stephen Crane in the West and Mexico. Edited by Joseph Katz. Kent, Ohio: Kent State Univ. Press, 1970.

Stephen Crane: Letters. Edited by R.W. Stallman and Lillian Gilkes. New York: New York Univ. Press, 1960.

Stephen Crane's Career: Perspectives and Evaluations.
    Edited by Thomas A. Gullason. New York: New York
    Univ. Press, 1972.
The War Dispatches of Stephen Crane. Edited by R.W. Stallman
    and E.R. Hagemann. New York: New York Univ. Press,
    1964.
Wolford, Chester L. *Stephen Crane, A Study of the Short
    Fiction.* Boston: Twayne Publishers, A Division of G.K.
    Hall & Co., 1989.

WEBSITES
The Red Badge of Courage Home Page, hosted by American Studies at the University of Virginia:
http://xroads.virginia.edu/~HYPER/CRANE/title.html

Stephen Crane Collection at Syracuse University:
http://libwww.syr.edu/information/spcollections/findingaids/HTML/crane.htm

Stephen Crane Papers at Columbia University:
http://www.columbia.edu/cu/libraries/indiv/rare/guides/Crane,S/index.html

The Stephen Crane Society Website:
http://www.gonzaga.edu/faculty/campbell/crane/index.html

Index